The Caribbean:
Its Implications for the United States
by
Virginia R. Domínguez
and Jorge I. Domínguez

CONTENTS

HEADLINE Series 253, February 1981   **$4.00**

Cover design: Hersch Wartik

The Authors

VIRGINIA R. DOMÍNGUEZ is assistant professor of anthropology at Duke University. She is author of *From Neighbor to Stranger: The Dilemma of Caribbean Peoples in the United States* (Yale, 1975) as well as articles on Caribbean migration to the United States and problems of racial, social and ethnic identity. She has done field work in New York City, Suriname and New Orleans, and historical research on Cuba and Puerto Rico.

JORGE I. DOMÍNGUEZ is professor of government and a member of the Center for International Affairs at Harvard University. He is the author of *Cuba: Order and Revolution* (Harvard Press, 1978), *Insurrection or Loyalty: The Breakdown of the Spanish American Empire* (Harvard Press, 1980), and other works. He is the president-elect of the Latin American Studies Association. Jorge Domínguez and his sister Virginia were born in Cuba.

We dedicate this joint work to Clara B. Carrera ('Mamama'), our maternal grandmother, in gratitude and love.

The Foreign Policy Association

The Foreign Policy Association is a private, nonprofit, nonpartisan educational organization. Its purpose is to stimulate wider interest and more effective participation in, and greater understanding of, world affairs among American citizens. Among its activities is the continuous publication, dating from 1935, of the HEADLINE Series pamphlets. The authors of these pamphlets are responsible for factual accuracy and for the views expressed. FPA itself takes no position on issues of United States foreign policy.

Preface

The exodus of 125,000 people from Cuba to Florida, the plight of the Haitian "boat people," military coups in Grenada and Suriname, the election defeat of Prime Minister Michael Manley's government in Jamaica—these were among the events that, at the outset of the 1980s, turned the attention of the government and people of the United States once more to the Caribbean.

To those of us who have been concerned with Caribbean affairs for many years, this resurrection of U.S. government interest in the region is both welcome and troubling. Welcome, because the fundamental problems faced by this region on our national doorstep—inhabited by over 30 million people in some 30 political units scattered across 800,000 square miles of sea—have for too long held an unwisely low priority in the policies of the United States. Troubling, because the U.S. government's reactions to recent trends in the region have conformed to an age-old pattern which experience has shown to be inadequate.

Traditionally, U.S. policy in the Caribbean, when it could be said to exist at all, has concentrated on short-term remedies designed to relax political tensions or to ward off perceived political or military threats. From the enunciation of the Monroe Doctrine in 1823 to the flurry of U.S. government activities that followed the 1979 coup in Grenada, successive episodes of U.S. concern over the region—rising at times to the level of virtual panic—have centered primarily on keeping any part of the Caribbean from "falling into the hands" of a rival power. Rarely has the United States given serious attention to long-range planning in the region or shown a serious interest in the problems of poverty and underdevelopment from which episodes of instability and political crisis in the Caribbean typically arise.

These defects of policy pose substantial dangers to U.S. interests, for this country is bound to the Caribbean by a dense web of geographic, strategic, social, economic and political circumstances. The circumstances, moreover, have been changing; military and strategic considerations have declined in importance and economic and demographic interactions have become far more significant. Yet the implications of these trends have thus far seemed only sporadically to reach the level of public—or even official—consciousness in this country. Indeed, most North Americans have barely even begun to realize the extent of the Caribbean presence in our own society. An estimated 4 million people of Caribbean birth or parentage now live on the U.S. mainland, and there is no reason to believe that this long-term migratory process is nearing its end. Not only does it pose new issues for U.S. immigration policy and for the domestic economy; it is also a symptom of unresolved problems in Caribbean economies and societies which, unless more effectively addressed, can damage U.S. economic and strategic interests in the region far more than any political ideology could do.

This essay argues, then, that it is in the best interests of the United States to help Caribbean countries cope more effectively with their economic and social problems and build a better life for their peoples. This, not military power, should be the primary focus and main instrument of a coherent, long-term U.S. policy for the Caribbean.

As background for our analysis of U.S. policy, we describe in the chapters that follow the historical roots from which today's Caribbean societies evolved, and the wide variety of social, economic and political entities that make up the Caribbean region today. Separate chapters discuss and compare the economies of the region, its political systems, and the increasingly important phenomenon of Caribbean emigration. Our final chapter examines the relationship between the Caribbean and the United States: its past, its present, the future we fear and the future we prefer.

Following scholarly tradition, we include in this study all the islands in the Caribbean Sea as well as the three Guianas (now known as Suriname, Guyana and French Guiana) and Belize—the last four being coastal states, recently or still under European sovereignty, which share with the islands a history of slavery and of export-propelled plantation economies, as well as an Afro-European cultural heritage. History has made these mainland territories as much a part of the Caribbean region as the islands themselves.

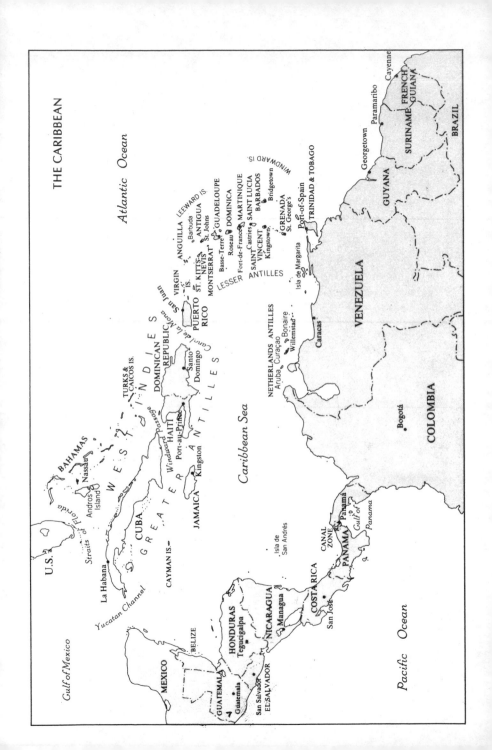

1

The Formation of Caribbean Societies

For nearly 500 years, the Caribbean has been a barometer of the Western world, reflecting the direction of social, economic, and political change in Europe and foretelling the nature of change in the Americas as a whole. The discovery of the New World began with the sighting of the Bahamas on October 12, 1492, and the first European settlement occurred shortly afterward on the Caribbean island of Hispaniola, now shared by Haiti and the Dominican Republic. The first experiments in sugarcane cultivation in the Americas took place also on Hispaniola before 1500. The first African slaves to cross the Atlantic in large numbers were transported to Hispaniola by 1506.

The Caribbean was also the earliest arena for the European rivalries that would dominate much of the history of the Western Hemisphere for centuries afterward. It was the gateway to the riches of the mainland and the provisioning ground for the Spanish fleets and the Northern European pirates. In few other parts of the world would the contrasts in economic policy between the Spanish Empire and its Northern European rivals become as glaring. While Spain concentrated on the extraction of precious metals from Mexico and Peru, the English, Dutch and

French soon turned from trading and raiding to intensive plantation agriculture. Spain controlled the Greater Antilles in the 16th and 17th centuries but did little to develop their agricultural potential. By contrast, the English, the Dutch, and the French colonized the much smaller islands of the Eastern Caribbean by the 1620s and 1630s, and within two generations transformed them into the greatest sugar-producing area in the world.

The decline of the Spanish Empire also surfaced in the Caribbean. Jamaica became English in 1655; the western third of Hispaniola became the French colony of Saint-Domingue (now Haiti) in 1697; the British briefly occupied Havana in 1762; the Spanish colony of Santo Domingo was overrun by Haitians during the protracted Haitian revolution at the turn of the 19th century. Cuba and Puerto Rico, Spain's last strongholds in the New World, came under U.S. hegemony as a result of the Spanish-American War of 1898.

The Caribbean's role as barometer of the Western world was social and ideological as well. Massive exploitation of enslaved Africans was a time bomb whose explosion set off the second successful independence movement in the New World, and led to the first black republic in the world—Haiti. The enslavement of Africans would be abolished by every major European power within a century of the Haitian revolution.

In the 20th century, the Caribbean has heralded the rise of U.S. economic power overseas, the passing of the surviving European empires, and the tensions of the cold war. Cuba and Puerto Rico were "freed" from the Spanish in 1898 only to come under U.S. hegemony in the aftermath. In 1915 U.S. Marines landed in Haiti, which remained under U.S. occupation until 1934. In 1917, the United States bought the Danish West Indies (Virgin Islands of the U.S.). In the Dominican Republic the United States, from 1905 to 1941, functioned as collector of customs and paymaster to European creditors; U.S. armed forces occupied the country from 1916 to 1924; and a second armed intervention took place in 1965.

The trend in recent decades, however, has been decolonization.

Jamaica and Trinidad and Tobago were granted independence from Britain in 1962. By 1979, seven more British colonies had gained independence: Barbados, Guyana, the Bahamas, Grenada, Dominica, St. Lucia and St. Vincent-Grenadines. Among islands of the Lesser Antilles still under the British flag, there are plans for the independence of Antigua, possibilities of independence for Montserrat and even for the tiny islands of St. Kitts, Nevis and Anguilla (see Table 1, p. 10).

The tensions of the cold war entered the Caribbean with the Cuban revolution of 1959. With it, the Caribbean became the site of the first Marxist-Leninist revolution in the Americas—a source of chronic concern in the United States. In addition, the governments of several recently independent countries are, or have recently been, explicitly left of center: Guyana, Jamaica, Suriname, St. Lucia and Grenada.

The historical ironies of U.S. reactions to events in the Caribbean are nowhere more evident than on the small island of Grenada. With a population estimated at about 100,000 in 1980, an area of 133 square miles, and nutmeg for its major export, it is not the most likely threat to a world power. Yet after the unexpected takeover of the government by the New Jewel Movement in March 1979, its demonstrative alignment with Cuba and the Soviet Union and its proclamations against capitalist control of developing countries by former colonial powers had immediate repercussions in Washington. U.S. policy-makers, noticing the tiny island nation for the first time, seemed to perceive it solely as a miniature symbol of the breakdown of *détente* and the spread of superpower rivalry in the third world.

Colonies of Exploitation

Today's Caribbean societies, with their resilience and vulnerability, bear the clear imprint of centuries of colonialism and slavery. History shows how the two served to maintain and maximize the exploitation of one group by another—of colonial subjects by colonial masters, and of slaves by colonial elites.

When Christopher Columbus reached the New World at the

Table 1

The Caribbean: Key Data

Country	Independence	Sovereign power	Est. pop. (thousands)	Percent annual increase[a]	Area (sq. km.)	Population density[b]	Infant deaths/1,000[c]	Female life expectancy
Antigua	—	U.K.	72	1.4	442	164	25	64
Bahamas	1973	U.K.	220	3.6	13,935	16	25	67
Barbados	1966	U.K.	254	1.0	431	590	28	67
Belize	—	U.K.	149	3.1	22,965	6	34	49
Bermuda	—	U.K.	57	1.3	53	1,069	19	72
British Virgin Islands	—	U.K.	12	2.6	153	78	19	55
Cayman Islands	—	U.K.	11	0.7	259	42	18	—
Cuba	1902	Spain, U.S.	9,596	1.7	114,524	84	23	72
Dominica	1978	U.K.	80	1.7	751	107	24	59
Dominican Republic	1844	Spain	4,978	2.9	48,734	102	44	59
French Guiana	—	France	60	—	91,000	1	43	—
Grenada	1974	U.K.	97	0.4	344	282	24	66
Guadeloupe	—	France	365	1.6	1,779	205	26	67
Guyana	1966	U.K.	827	2.4	214,969	4	51	63
Haiti	1804	France	4,749	1.6	27,750	171	—	51
Jamaica	1962	U.K.	2,085	1.6	10,991	190	21	67
Martinique	—	France	374	1.5	1,102	339	19	67
Montserrat	—	U.K.	13	2.1	98	133	49	55
Netherlands Antilles	—	Neth.	252	—	873	286	20	66
Puerto Rico	—	U.S.	3,303	2.8	8,897	371	19	76
St. Kitts-Nevis-Anguilla	—	U.K.	66	0.4	357	185	41	62
St. Lucia	1979	U.K.	112	1.5	616	182	37	58
St. Vincent-Grenadines	1979	U.K.	100	—	388	258	100	60
Suriname	1975	Neth.	448	2.7	163,265	3	31	67
Trinidad and Tobago	1962	U.K.	1,110	—	5,128	220	27	68
Turks and Caicos Islands	—	U.K.	6	—	430	14	32	—
U.S. Virgin Islands	—	U.S.	100	—	344	291	25	—
United States	1776	U.K.	216,817	0.8	9,363,123	23	14	77

a. 1970-77. b. Estimates for mid-year 1977. c. Information compiled from selected years, 1970s.

Source: *UN Statistical Yearbook* (1978)

end of the 15th century, the islands of the Caribbean were inhabited by two American Indian groups, Arawaks and Caribs, that had migrated from northern South America. By the end of the 18th century, the Arawak population was extinct and the small-island Caribs were reduced to a few hundred survivors, mostly of mixed ancestry, in the mountain hideouts—the name Caribbean remaining as their only monument. The Europeans had needed labor to turn raw material into capital for repatriation to Europe, but the American Indians were neither numerous enough, nor resistant enough to disease, nor pliable enough, to serve their purpose.

With the disappearance of the American Indians, the road was open for a transformation that would make the Caribbean significantly different from almost all other colonies in history. European colonization had been of two types. Almost everywhere else in the world. In the thinly populated wilderness of North America and Australia, Europeans established colonies of settlement—extensions of European society in which the colonists did their own work while the less numerous indigenous peoples were either killed off or relegated to the hinterland. In most of Central and South America, as well as colonial Asia and Africa, Europeans established colonies of conquest—forming a ruling European elite while the conquered indigenous majorities provided the labor force. But in the Caribbean, Europeans established productive colonies using neither their own labor nor that of the indigenous population. To exploit the agricultural and mineral potential of the region, Europeans *imported* vast numbers of forced laborers while they themselves became the colonial elite. Exploitation of natural and human resources, rather than settlement or conquest, became the trademark of most Caribbean islands.

Much of the arable land of the region was turned over to sugarcane cultivation. Instead of small- or medium-sized farms producing a variety of crops for internal consumption or a limited external market, large plantations dominated the economy of most of the Caribbean as early as the 17th century. The

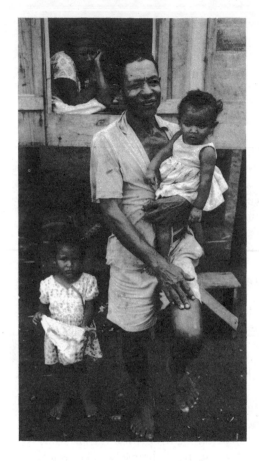

A Carib family—among the few survivors of the American Indian group for whom the region is named—in Dominica

Bernard Pierre Wolff

plantations which concentrated on the production of sugarcane for the European market grew as the demand for sugar rose in the expanding factory cities of Europe. The tropical climate and the backbreaking labor needed for sugar production on these plantations did little to attract voluntary European labor. Hence, European colonial powers turned to forced labor to develop the agricultural potential of the region.

It is estimated that more than 250,000 English and French indentured laborers were sent to man European plantations in the Lesser Antilles in the early stages of colonization. And millions of enslaved Africans were imported into the Caribbean for the same purposes during nearly four centuries. This forced emigration was surely one of the most colossal demographic events of modern times. Some recent cautious estimates reveal its extent. The French colony of Saint-Domingue imported 790,000 slaves in 90 years; the British colony of Jamaica received 662,000 slaves in 109 years; and Spanish America (consisting essentially of Cuba and Puerto Rico) received 606,000 slaves between 1811 and 1870.

As the slave trade dwindled in the mid-19th century, plantation owners sought substitutes for slaves among the nonwhite and the indentured. Cuba, for example, imported Chinese and Mexican Indian workers. Even after slavery was abolished (first in the 1830s in the British Caribbean, lastly in 1886 in Cuba), much of the labor was foreign and indentured. The Dutch in Suriname imported East Indians until the British discontinued this form of emigration from India in 1917, then turned to Dutch-ruled Java, their main source well into the 1930s. East Indians also went to Guyana and Trinidad in large numbers, and to Jamaica in smaller numbers. Not until the 20th century did the Caribbean cease to import large numbers of non-European workers to man the huge agro-industrial complex of its export-propelled economies.

The Experience of Slavery

The treatment of enslaved workers had a profound effect on Caribbean societies. The plantations of the Lesser Antilles were generally owned by absentee landlords and run by white overseers. Few whites lived on most of these islands after the middle of the 17th century, and fewer still considered the Caribbean their home. Correspondingly, the slaves were treated as instruments of production, rather than as subjects, citizens, or even dependents. So long as slaves could be easily and inexpensively replaced before the abolition of the slave trade, it was considered more profitable to import slaves than to raise them. Slave conditions were, therefore, abominable. The average length of life for a Guyanese slave in the early 19th century was under 23 years. Although 4 million Africans were sold into the British, French, and Dutch Caribbean during colonial times, there were no more than a million and a half persons of African descent in these territories when slavery ended. Half of those Africans who migrated into the islands to replace dying slaves themselves perished during the first three years of life in the Caribbean.

The slave system in the Spanish colonies of the Greater Antilles, although the first to begin, was considerably less severe, for the first 300 years of colonization, than under the other European powers. There was less systematic cruelty and more manumission (freeing of slaves) and miscegenation (intermarriage of whites and blacks). There is some evidence that the Spanish crown and the Catholic Church saw themselves as protectors of African slaves in the New World. But in the 19th century, the treatment of slaves on the Spanish Caribbean's sugar plantations was as harsh as it had ever been in the Lesser Antilles. It was then that Cuba's sugar industry grew in importance on the world market as the result of changes in Spanish economic policy. Manumission became less frequent; excessive punishment, more prevalent; and precautions against loss of slave runaways, more efficient. Puerto Rico underwent a similar transformation. Before the 19th century, it had been little more than a military outpost and provisioning station. Its population was sparse and there were far more whites than slaves. Then came the boom in sugar production. Between 1787 and 1846 the population of the island more than quadrupled, and the slave sector was up from 11,260 to 51,265. Slaves were imported despite the official abolition of the slave trade. Indeed, the labor needs of Puerto Rican plantation owners were so great that, beginning in 1824, free but landless white agricultural workers were subjected to a system of forced labor.

The memory of Caribbean slavery escapes few in the Caribbean. Fewer than 10 percent of the people of the British, French, and Dutch Caribbean today are white. The rest, the vast

A plantation owner and slave, from a German engraving in the Culver Pictures collection

majority, are descended from indentured or enslaved workers. In the Spanish Caribbean, a smaller percentage of the population is black, but a higher percentage is of mixed racial ancestry. These people, too, carry the stigma of a slave past.

Color discrimination within the Caribbean is itself a legacy of the slave system. Slaves were non-Europeans; slave owners, whites or at least in part descended from whites. Thus, dark skin became symbolic of low status, and white skin, symbolic of high status. It is one of the ironies of the Caribbean that miscegenation strengthened rather than undermined this equation. Throughout the region, the children of white men and slave women were accorded special status. If they remained slaves, it was as household servants and semi-independent craftsmen, almost never as field slaves. Many were taught to read and write; many were publicly acknowledged by their white fathers. Often, however, they were freed at birth, raised in the master's household, and educated in European schools. Many of these "free-colored" inherited landed property and slaves to go with the property. Their legal and social status, like their physical appearance, was closer to that of whites than was the case among black slaves.

Yet the free-colored were always in an ambiguous position. Though they turned to whites for models of behavior, whites suspected them as a group and kept them partly disenfranchised. Throughout the Caribbean, whites periodically suspected the free-colored of aiding and abetting slaves; yet the social system made most free-colored more obsessed with the process of "whitening" for the sake of upward mobility than with the plight of black slaves. Thus, miscegenation simply reinforced the social order established by European planters and African slaves, and allowed color stratification to persist long after the abolition of slavery.

Success in resisting slavery enabled the Caribbean people to emerge from the experience of colonialism with a rare sense of pride. With the exception of French Saint-Domingue, where slaves freed themselves through revolution, Africans and their descendants throughout the region resisted the oppression of slavery through periodic uprisings and often through subterfuge. Where the terrain allowed it, as in the densely forested Guianas or in mountainous Jamaica and eastern Cuba, they ran away. The six tribes of descendants of runaway slaves in the interior of Suriname today, and the ever-present trickster figure in much of Afro-Caribbean folklore, stand as living symbols of slave resistance. Caribbeans today take pride in these memories, and in having created out of disparate African, Asian and European elements a new Caribbean society and culture with a distinctive Afro-American flavor.

This history is reflected in a multiplicity of Caribbean languages. Brought to the New World from all over West and Central Africa, the slaves had no common language. Out of the need to communicate with both masters and slaves, they combined elements of European and African languages to give birth to the French-based Creole languages of Haiti, Martinique, Guadeloupe and Dominica; the English-based Sranan (or Taki-Taki) and Djukatongo of Suriname; the English Creole of Jamaica; and the Portuguese-based Saramakatongo of Suriname and Papiamentu of the Netherlands Antilles. Only in the Spanish Caribbean, where the ratio of whites to blacks was far greater than elsewhere in the region, did a Creole language fail to develop among the masses of slaves.

In adapting European religions, Africans and their descendants were equally creative. Dahomean religion and French Catholicism combined to form a rich complex of beliefs and rituals now known as Haitian voodoo. In Cuba, Puerto Rico and the Dominican Republic, Spanish Catholicism combined with Yoruba and Lucumi religions to produce Santería and Nañiguismo. In the English and Dutch Caribbean, Moravian Evangelicalism, Anglicanism, Roman Catholicism and Pentecostalism today experience the impact of West African religious beliefs and rituals. The elites and the middle classes decry these influences as desecration of their European religions, but often influences from African religions appear at the very top of the socioeconomic ladder. Hinduism and Islam have flourished, too, especially in the Guianas and Trinidad.

In sum, at the heart of the history of the Caribbean is the history of colonialism and of reactions to colonialism; of slavery and indentured servitude and resistance to them; of exploitation and attempts to preserve human dignity in the face of exploitation. If Caribbean peoples are proud, it is because they managed to be creative when they were not even expected to survive.

2

The Caribbean Today

Widely shared experiences helped shape the individual Caribbean countries. But in their histories, their geography, and their social, political, and economic circumstances there are also features unique to each country. This chapter will discuss separately the main countries and groups of countries (see Table 1).

Cuba

The Republic of Cuba consists of the island of Cuba, the Isle of Youth (formerly the Isle of Pines) and a great many small cays that are sparsely inhabited or uninhabited. The largest of the islands of the Caribbean, Cuba has about one-third of the population of the entire region; but because of its size, its population density by Caribbean standards is low.

Almost to the end of the 19th century, long after the vast Spanish Empire on the American mainland was gone, Spain clung to its Caribbean colonies—including Cuba, "the pearl of the Antilles." Much of the 19th-century history of Cuba is a chronicle of nationalist uprisings which the Spanish governors countered at times with liberalizing reforms, at times with brutal repression.

Repeatedly, some Cubans appealed for aid to the United States. Before the U.S. Civil War, pro-slavery forces in this country attempted at times to engineer the annexation of Cuba as a slave state. After slavery ended in both countries, the matter took a different turn. In 1898, when a new wave of Cuban insurgency, begun in 1895, led the United States to war with Spain, the United States forswore annexation and backed Cuban independence. This independence was qualified, however, by the long-term lease of Guantánamo Bay for a major U.S. military and naval base, and especially by a virtual U.S. protectorate that lasted until 1934. Fulgencio Batista ruled Cuba, directly or through surrogates, from 1933 to 1944, and again, from 1952 through 1958, with a civilian and relatively democratic interlude in the intervening years. Until the late 1950s Cuba was of interest to the United States chiefly as the site of the Guantánamo base, as a tourist resort and center for trade and investment.

The revolution led by Fidel Castro, which overthrew the Batista government in 1959, was the major event of Cuba's history in the 20th century. The revolutionary government has radically altered Cuba's international position and reorganized many aspects of Cuban national life.

In its international relations, Cuba under Castro has devoted much of its energy to supporting what it sees as anticolonial, anti-imperialist and, inevitably, anti-U.S. revolutions—at first only in Latin America, but more recently farther afield. In keeping with its political orientation, it has become closely aligned with the Soviet Union, especially since the early 1970s. The Soviet Union has provided considerable military, economic and other kinds of aid to Cuba without which the Cuban revolutionary government could not have survived. In turn, Cuba and the Soviet Union have cooperated closely in a number of overseas military ventures. The most dramatic among these have been their decisive military participation on the winning side in the Angolan civil war (1975-76), and their defeat of the Somali invasion of the Ogaden region of Ethiopia in 1978. Cuba committed tens of thousands of troops to these overseas wars—relative to population, a commitment comparable to that of the

United States in Vietnam at the peak of that war. Other aspects of Cuban foreign relations have helped to make that country a leading actor in world affairs. In 1979 President Castro, despite his country's overt alignment with Moscow, was elected to a three-year term as chairman of the Nonaligned Movement that includes about a hundred countries. Cuban foreign policy is also active in the promotion of its cultural, artistic and literary goals—a world of the arts with a revolutionary commitment— through its mass media, the holding of international meetings, contests and awards, and participation in international organizations. The extent of this activity is striking for such a small country.

At home, the revolutionary government has chosen a centralized strategy toward politics, economics and society. This centralization stemmed in part from threats to the revolutionary regime in the early 1960s, but more from the choices and preferences of the leadership—and especially of Fidel Castro, the decisive figure in Cuba's national life of the past quarter-century. By the 1970s, however, Castro's personal leadership had been supplemented by an elaborate set of organizations to formulate and carry out policy. Of these, the most important is the Communist party of Cuba—the only party that can operate legally. The party, in turn, guides and monitors the work of a panoply of mass organizations—for labor, peasants, students, women and neighborhood groups—as well as the work of the organs of government.

Cuba's economy is also highly centralized. Private ownership of the means of production has virtually disappeared outside of a minority in the agricultural sector. The government ministries and state enterprises are responsible for the conduct of most economic affairs. Under this system aggregate economic growth has been negligible. Severe economic crises occurred in the early 1960s, in the late 1960s (the worst of all), and in 1980. The only period of sustained growth occurred in the first half of the 1970s, thanks in part to a rise in world prices of sugar, the product on which Cuba still depends for four-fifths of its foreign exchange.

If the revolution's growth strategy has failed, its distribution strategy has succeeded. Income inequality, marked before the revolution, has been narrowed substantially. Many basic necessities have been provided to the people, bringing considerable improvements in the health and education of the majority. Food and medicines remain rationed, but the commitment to equitable distribution of scarce essential resources has been honored. Housing, on the other hand, remains seriously inadequate, as does mass transportation—two of the conspicuous failures of the revolutionary government.

Citizen participation has been an important feature of political life in Cuba. For the bulk of these years, however, political mobilization of the citizenry to carry out the wishes of the leadership has been the principal, and often the only, type of participation permitted.

Some relaxation occurred in the 1970s, when the government began to permit, and even to stimulate, more independent participation in local political affairs. Citizens now do complain more readily about everyday problems in their local communities. But the central government retains considerable power to decide how to cope with such complaints. In 1980, the government tightened some of the mechanisms of internal security that had been loosened in the 1970s. These developments—along with the severe economic crisis—partly explain the departure of 125,000 Cubans to the United States in a period of a few weeks in 1980.

The Cuban revolutionary government thus entered the 1980s still strong but troubled at home, and overcommitted overseas. Its strength derived from its considerable past accomplishments and the substantial popular support it still retained. But it remains to be seen how long even the largest of the Caribbean islands can behave as if it were a world power when so many needs of its own people are still unmet.

The Dominican Republic and Haiti

The Dominican Republic and Haiti occupy the eastern and western parts, respectively, of the island of Hispaniola. While they are comparable in population, Haiti is more crowded because its area is smaller. These two neighbors have been barely able to coexist on this island since independence. Suspicion and fear have been bred by differences in culture, in language (Spanish in the Dominican Republic, Creole and French in Haiti), and in physical appearance (Haiti is overwhelmingly black, while the Dominican Republic has a mulatto majority and a significant white minority). Their histories in the 20th century have also been profoundly affected by their relations with the United States, which occupied both countries militarily in the earlier decades of the century.

The **Dominican Republic** was dominated by General Rafael Leónidas Trujillo from 1930 until his assassination in 1961. The U.S. government intervened repeatedly after Trujillo's death to seek to guarantee a transition to civilian rule through competitive elections and to ward off military coups. A social reformer, Juan Bosch, won the December 1962 elections and became president early in 1963, but was overthrown by a military junta late in that year. Early in 1965 an effort by an opposition group to overthrow this military government's successors and to restore Bosch to the presidency led to a division in the Dominican armed forces. The U.S. government—afraid that these events could provide an opening for the establishment of a "second Cuba" in the Caribbean—intervened with U.S. troops on April 28, 1965, eventually occupying the country.

The U.S. military occupation, authorized after the fact by the Organization of American States, was accompanied also by considerable U.S. economic and military aid and by efforts to restructure the Dominican political system. The U.S. forces withdrew in 1966 after presidential elections led to the victory of Joaquín Balaguer, who had served the Trujillo regime long and closely in several leading positions. Reelected twice, Balaguer was defeated in his bid for a fourth term by Antonio Guzmán in 1978. Even then, the U.S. government had to intervene diplomatically to make certain that the election count would proceed accurately and fairly.

In short, the United States has played a fundamental role in contemporary Dominican history. It is an essential power factor that shapes and reshapes Dominican political life. Moreover, few countries' economies are so closely linked to that of the United States.

The Dominican Republic's economic growth rate during most of the 1970s was excellent and, during the first half of the decade, ranked close to the top among the world's non-oil-producing countries. However, it still has serious problems of economic inequality. While considerable improvements have occurred toward meeting the basic needs of the people, the task ahead remains formidable.

The history of **Haiti** in recent times has been troubled. After U.S. forces were withdrawn in the mid-1930s, the country was ruled by an oligarchy until the 1950s. Years of instability led in 1957 to the dictatorship of François ("Papa Doc") Duvalier. His regime was so perniciously despotic, brutal to its people, rapacious in its policies toward the country's resources, and fundamentally uninterested in change, that the U.S. government eventually stopped all assistance to it. Haiti's economic performance during the 1960s was among the world's worst. Its real per capita income, already the lowest in the hemisphere, worsened steadily; moreover, inequality in the distribution of income probably worsened.

Even today, Haiti remains the poorest country of the hemisphere by virtually every measure. Some of the Haitian government's more gruesome terroristic practices abated upon François Duvalier's death in 1971 and the succession of his son, Jean-Claude, but the combination of a disastrous social and economic situation and political repression persists—and explains the desperate flight of so many Haitians, illegally, to the United States.

Jean-Claude Duvalier's government has, however, shown some willingness to change. Haiti's economic growth rate has improved considerably, although it is still not much ahead of population growth. The United States has resumed economic and military aid to Haiti. While the sums are not large relative to the country's population, they represent a substantial portion of

Haiti's international economic resources. Haiti has also benefited from improved world coffee prices, has stimulated tourism and production of minerals, and has welcomed subsidiaries of U.S. manufacturing enterprises which use low-wage Haitian labor to produce exports which receive preferential tariff treatment in the United States.

Thus both Haiti and the Dominican Republic find their histories, and probably their futures, inextricably tied to the United States. The United States affects much of the rhythm of their politics. Its trade, aid and investment are decisive for the fate of both economies. And it receives as immigrants or refugees an unceasing stream of Dominicans and Haitians who prefer to live as strangers in a foreign land rather than suffer at home.

The English-speaking 'Giants'

The hundreds of islands that once made up Britain's Caribbean empire are now grouped into 17 political units, ten of which had attained independence by 1979. Of these ten, four are the key countries of the English-speaking Caribbean: Jamaica, Barbados, Trinidad and Tobago, and Guyana (a coastal state). They became independent between 1962 and 1966 after the collapse of the West Indies Federation, which had included the first three as well as smaller English-speaking islands of the region. Of the four, the densely populated island republics of Jamaica, and Trinidad and Tobago, have the most people; Guyana has the largest land area but much of it is tropical rain forest. Barbados, the smallest in both population and area, is nonetheless the giant of the Lesser Antilles.

In their political constitutions, all these countries—as has been normal for former British colonies belonging to the Commonwealth—adopted Britain's "Westminster model" of parliamentary government. At the head of the government is a prime minister, nominally appointed by the British crown but legally responsible to the national Parliament. The ways in which this system has functioned in the four countries, however, has varied greatly in response to their different societies.

Ethnically, Jamaica and Barbados are fairly homogeneous,

with blacks in the overwhelming majority and Europeans and people of mixed-race, small minorities. Color differences, however, favor the minorities: the lighter the skin, the higher the status is likely to be.

The ethnic composition of Guyana and Trinidad and Tobago is much more complex, reflecting their history of indentured labor. Guyana has an East Indian majority that has thus far had limited access to political power; leaders of the minority black community (somewhat over a third of the population) have thus far held the key levers of power. The blacks also dominate the politics of Trinidad and Tobago, where they are in the majority, with East Indians making up about three-eighths of the population. In both countries the East Indians are divided along general

Sugarcane plantation workers in Haiti

caste lines and between Hindu and Muslim religious communities, making it difficult for them to act in concert.

The ethnic divisions in Trinidad and Tobago and in Guyana have had an enormous impact on the politics of these countries. The major political forces draw their strength and electoral support from one ethnic community or another. Those in power are generally reluctant to allow the fully free interplay of social forces not only for fear they would lose power but also because of a concern that conflict in such deeply divided societies could be explosive. This political-cultural rigidity is one key explanation for the fact that, since independence, only Eric Williams has been prime minister of Trinidad and Tobago, and only Forbes Burnham has been prime minister of Guyana. In the latter case, coercion and intimidation over the opposition increased as the 1980s opened.

In economic affairs, these two countries are markedly different. In the 1970s Trinidad and Tobago benefited from its petroleum resources and industries to become the most economically viable Caribbean economy—while in Guyana, bauxite and sugar production, its key items, actually declined during most of the 1970s. Trinidad and Tobago saw the possibility and, for some of its people, the reality of economic prosperity—whereas Guyana made little progress even in meeting basic necessities. The government of Trinidad and Tobago played an important role in regulating its economy but allowed considerable room for private enterprise—while Guyana attempted even more government economic intervention under its brand of "cooperative socialism."

In Jamaica and Barbados, more ethnically homogeneous, the British model of government has worked not only in form but in substance. The cabinet depends on its parliamentary majority, and that in turn depends on winning vigorously contested elections in single-member districts. Power has passed in both Barbados and Jamaica not only from one prime minister to the next within the same party, but also from government to opposition party at least once since independence, most recently in October 1980 in Jamaica. Jamaica, however, has been plagued also by a great deal of violence, much of it related to political competition. Civil violence will have to be restrained in the future if Jamaican democracy is to survive.

In economic terms, Jamaica fared poorly during most of the 1970s. Prime Minister Michael Manley, determined to provide badly needed but costly social services to the people, imposed fiscal and export policies which incurred the wrath of the business community. The nation came close to bankruptcy despite a considerable flow of aid from the United States and Western Europe and, later, from the Soviet Union, Eastern Europe and Cuba. Relations with Washington suffered as a result. Manley's policies were a main issue in the 1980 election in which Edward Seaga, a champion of private enterprise and foreign investment, won decisively. It remains to be seen how well the new government will succeed in dealing with Jamaica's social and economic difficulties.

Barbados' economic performance has been better and steadier than Jamaica's, but also insufficient to meet the needs of its people. Barbados has allowed greater play to private business firms, national and multinational. It too has drawn closer to the United States.

Puerto Rico

The Commonwealth of Puerto Rico is a state "freely associated" with the United States. It has been a U.S. possession since the United States defeated Spain in 1898. Under the commonwealth statute adopted in 1952, Puerto Rico elects its own governor and legislature. Its people are U.S. citizens and may travel without passports to and from the U.S. mainland, where some 2 million of them reside. Puerto Ricans are exempt from U.S. income taxes but are eligible for most of the health, education and welfare payments available to mainlanders. Such are the chief benefits of commonwealth status. On the debit side, Puerto Ricans have no vote in U.S. national elections, no voting representatives in the U.S. Congress, a far lower per capita income than mainlanders (although high by Caribbean standards) and no sovereign national existence of their own.

The politics of political status have long held center stage in the island's affairs. Puerto Rican political parties have debated the issue for most of this century. Some argue that Puerto Rico should join the United States as the 51st state; others that it should become independent; and still others that it should continue its commonwealth status, or some variant thereof. In the November 1980 gubernatorial elections, the pro-commonwealth and pro-statehood parties were virtually tied, with the latter the winner by a few thousand votes; pro-independence parties received less than 5 percent of the votes cast. As a result, a plebiscite on statehood, scheduled for 1981, was postponed indefinitely.

The question of Puerto Rico's status is of obvious importance in a political and economic sense, but it is more than that. It affects the nature of the island's culture, the standing of the Spanish language, the policies to be followed in schools at all levels, the programming shown over radio and television—in short, the content and symbols of national identity. Puerto Ricans are perhaps the only people in Latin America for whom matters of core national identity remain unsettled.

A major figure in Puerto Rican contemporary history was the late Luis Muñoz Marín, the founder of the long-dominant Popular Democratic party. He designed the basis for the commonwealth agreement, implemented in the early 1950s and subsequently modified. It was also Muñoz Marín who designed the country's economic strategy, described later, that was spectacularly successful in some but not all respects. That economic strategy has been emulated to some degree by many other Caribbean countries. That fact, plus the presence of the United States as the sovereign power, are determining factors in Puerto Rico's role in the Caribbean.

Puerto Rican politics reached another turning point in 1964 when Muñoz Marín announced his retirement as governor after a quarter-century in power. In an example of statesmanship unique in the Caribbean—and not common anywhere—he chose to step down because he believed it politically unhealthy for his party and his people to depend so much on one man. One consequence of that decision was to break his party's dominance on the island's politics. No governor after him was elected to more than one term until 1980, when Carlos Romero Barceló was reelected by a very narrow margin. Such a degree of political competitiveness and equilibrium, along with high electoral participation, is also rare in Caribbean politics.

Along with that rapid rotation of top officeholders, however, there has been a spreading political malaise in Puerto Rico from the late 1960s onward. It stems from two sources: the slowdown in what had seemed ever-increasing prosperity, and renewed doubt about the island's ties to the United States. The result has been a weakening of support for the commonwealth option; yet neither of the other alternatives has mustered enough support to provide a more permanent solution to the problem of status.

The Caribbean 'Crowd'

Beyond the most populous countries, the Caribbean region includes a score of others—ranging from Suriname and Belize on the mainland, large in area but thinly populated, to small island countries crowded with people, such as Martinique, Grenada or St. Lucia. None has more than a half-million people; some have only a few thousand.

Most of these small countries are still European dependencies, but several have already become independent, and most of the others, chief among them being Belize and the Netherlands Antilles, are on the path toward independence. The island territories of Guadeloupe and Martinique and the mainland territory of French Guiana, originally French colonies, were made departments of France in 1946—much as Hawaii is a state of the United States—and elect their own delegates to the French national assembly.

All of these territories have considerable poverty. A few, such as Belize and Suriname, have substantial natural resources, but the job of exploiting them remains to be done. Suriname's production of its key export, bauxite, actually declined in the 1970s.

Their economic weakness makes most of these territories

highly dependent on outside aid, especially from the present or former colonial powers; but the volume of this aid varies widely. France provides heavy subsidies to its Caribbean departments, far exceeding in per capita terms the aid that any other outside power gives to any country in the region except for Soviet aid to Cuba. The Netherlands provides considerable per capita resources to the Netherlands Antilles and even more to its former colony, Suriname. Britain's aid to its colonies and former colonies is meager by comparison.

Political life in this Caribbean "crowd" varies widely. St. Lucia and Dominica follow the Westminster model and have each witnessed at least one peaceful transfer of political power from government to opposition parties since they became independent. At the other end of the spectrum, Grenada endured the increasingly capricious and arbitrary rule of Prime Minister Eric Gairy from independence until his overthrow in 1979 by forces that later aligned with Cuba—an event which brought a stronger response from Washington than might have been expected in view of its small size and meager resources.

Suriname, the only Dutch Caribbean colony to have gained independence so far, contains the richest mosaic of peoples anywhere in the region. While a multi-party coalition was able to rule for a while after independence, a series of military coups rocked the country in 1980. These began with a mutiny by noncommissioned officers over the army's pay and continued for several months as personalities, ideologies, and fiefdoms were sorted out. Suriname's political future is clouded by the combination of extreme ethnic, linguistic and religious fragmentation with the most rampant military praetorianism in the region.

The troubles of these smaller and more obscure countries could well draw the United States further into involvement in the Caribbean. Mention has been made of the impact of the Grenadian revolution. Other trouble spots of a more traditional sort also persist. Some of the boundaries of French Guiana, Suriname and Guyana remain undefined; some of the settlements reached thus far have been subsequently questioned. Belize's independence has been long delayed by its people's fear of invasion by Guatemala, which lays claim to the entire territory on the argument that the British stole it in the 19th century. Guatemala appears willing to settle for some substantial portion of Belize's southern territory, but Belize insists on preserving its territorial integrity.

More than one small island-group state is threatened with secession by islands within the group—the same process of fragmentation that has doomed regional integration since the collapse of the West Indies Federation. St. Vincent-Grenadines was faced with a secessionist effort by Union Island in 1979, prevented only by a military intervention by Barbados. Secessionism is a core political issue, too, in Trinidad and Tobago, St. Kitts-Nevis-Anguilla and the Netherlands Antilles, among others. Thus the likelihood of armed conflict, often for the most traditional of reasons, casts a pall on the Caribbean crowd.

3

Contemporary
Caribbean Economies

Caribbean economies have changed little in their basic structure since the days of plantation slavery. Virtually all still depend mainly on the production of raw materials (or services, chiefly tourism) for export. Nearly all must import capital and technology from industrialized nations in order to compete on the world market. Few are diversified enough to withstand catastrophe when the world price of their main export commodity drops severely. Most are dominated by large enterprises (private or public) which claim to achieve added efficiency through economies of scale. Traditional small businesses and peasant producers constitute a small sector of Caribbean economies and account for an even smaller share of export income. The great majority of the countries, including revolutionary Cuba, depend on one or two industrialized nations to buy half or more of their exports and to sell them most of the products they import (see Table 2, p. 34). And in nearly all, ironically, a large percentage of the food the people eat is imported.

Some aspects of Caribbean economies are, of course, fixed. Most of the islands are very small. They are handicapped by an awkward distribution of natural resources. The Bahamas have enormous supplies of salt, but little drinkable water. Cuba is the world's fifth largest exporter of nickel, and Jamaica produces more bauxite than any other country in the world except Australia, but both must import petroleum. Trinidad has vast reserves of oil and natural gas, but little land on which to grow food for its growing population. A surprisingly large share of the land in the Caribbean, in fact, is ill-suited for most agricultural crops. And the region is plagued by yearly hurricanes.

For much of the region, the answer to these difficulties has been the same for centuries: sugar. Sugarcane is a hardy crop. Several high-yielding varieties adapt well to the Caribbean's ecological conditions. Sugarcane maintains soil fertility, survives most floods and hurricanes and resists many pests and diseases. Once an area has been turned over to sugarcane cultivation, there is often reluctance to switch to a less-dependable crop. And many of those who do experiment on previously uncultivated land still plant sugarcane on the old land for security. As a result, there is little production of food crops for the internal Caribbean market. Even landless agricultural workers and sharecroppers, when given small plots of land for vegetable gardening, often grow sugarcane instead.

The Decline of Sugar

The long-term trend, however, has been away from sugar. Increasingly in the last century, many of the smaller islands stopped trying to compete with the booming European beet sugar industry or with the larger cane producers in Louisiana, Cuba and Brazil, and turned to growing cotton, spices, bananas, citrus fruits, coconuts or pineapples.

Most larger countries of the region, in fact, have been turning away from agriculture altogether. As recently as 1938, agricultural production accounted for 36 percent of Jamaica's gross domestic product (GDP); by 1972, for only 9 percent. Mining and, to a lesser degree, tourism have become Jamaica's main income earners. In Trinidad and Tobago, it is estimated that petroleum now contributes 45 percent of the national product, 60 percent of the government revenue, and 90 percent of foreign earnings. In Suriname, the mining of bauxite has taken center

Table 2

Direction of International Trade in 1976

Countries	Top two suppliers (percentage of total imports)		Top two customers (percentage of total exports)	
Bahamas	Saudi Arabia	45	U.S.	94
	Libyan Arab Rep.	12	U.K.	1
Barbados	U.S.	24	U.S.	31
	U.K.	19	Ireland	14
Belize	U.S.	39	U.S.	51
	U.K.	22	U.K.	41
Bermuda	U.S.	52	U.S.	14
	U.K.	12	U.K.	7
Cuba	U.S.S.R.	40	U.S.S.R.	56
	Japan	12	Spain	8
Dominican Republic	U.S.	48	U.S.	70
	Netherlands Antilles	16	Switzerland	8
Guadeloupe	France	74	France	84
	U.S.	5	Martinique	11
Guyana	U.S.	29	U.K.	27
	U.K.	23	U.S.	20
Haiti	U.S.	56	U.S.	67
	Netherlands Antilles	7	France	10
Jamaica	U.S.	37	U.S.	41
	Venezuela	15	U.K.	18
Martinique	France	61	France	68
	Germany	8	Guadeloupe	3
Netherlands Antilles	Venezuela	45	U.S.	47
	Saudi Arabia	34	Ecuador	5
Suriname	U.S.	36	U.S.	34
	Netherlands	13	U.K.	14
Trinidad and	Saudi Arabia	26	U.S.	69
Tobago	U.S.	20	U.K.	5

Source: *UN Statistical Yearbook* (1978)

stage away from sugar production. Suriname is the fourth largest producer of bauxite in the world. Islands less blessed with mineral resources have turned to manufacturing, tourism and financial services. Aruba and Curaçao refine petroleum; Barbados has a growing clothing industry; Puerto Rico is dotted with assembly plants; the Cayman Islands offer financial services; all depend heavily on tourism. The decline of agriculture is most marked on the island of Puerto Rico, where agriculture contributed only 3 percent of the GDP by 1973, and manufacturing 26 percent.

The benefits of the shift into manufacturing have been limited. Manufacturing in the Caribbean for the most part combines local labor with imported capital, since most Caribbean countries simply cannot accumulate enough national savings for large capital investments. Thus, most of the profit generated by manufacturing in, for example, the Netherlands Antilles or Puerto Rico, leaves the islands along with the source of capital. The islands gain, of course, in fiscal revenues, employment, purchases of local products and in other ways, but their gains are limited mainly to whatever price the foreign entrepreneur will pay for their labor. What the Netherlands Antilles and Puerto Rico have essentially done, then, is to shift from the export of agricultural goods to the export of labor.

Worsening Unemployment

To make matters worse, the Caribbean, with its growing population, suffers from a long-term shift throughout the region in the mix of land, labor and capital. Sugarcane production has always been labor-intensive, and throughout the colonial period the Caribbean was rich in land but short on labor for the cane fields. But the population of the Caribbean began to grow significantly by the middle of the 19th century as slavery was abolished and public health measures and the treatment of tropical diseases improved. Coinciding with this natural growth came the decline of the sugar industry, first in much of the Lesser Antilles. The newly freed population became peasants and sharecroppers on the available lands, and supplemented their income by seasonal work on the plantations. But as agricultural capital sought to economize, sugar planters mechanized and modernized at the expense of labor. Seasonal, rather than full-time employment, became the norm. The land-labor problem which had dominated centuries of Caribbean economic history was reversed, with labor now in surplus.

The worst of the surplus labor problem has surfaced only recently with the shift away from agriculture. The new exporting industries are for the most part capital-intensive, not labor-intensive. Jamaican mining, for example, contributed 13 percent of the country's GDP in 1973 but employed only 1.3 percent of the labor force. Jamaica's tourist industry employed only about 12,000 people. By contrast, agriculture, forestry and fishing, which contributed only 8 percent of the GDP, employed 35 percent of the labor force. The same pattern, though less skewed, obtains as well in Trinidad and Tobago.

The decline in employment in the traditional agricultural sectors and the low levels of employment provided by the new exporting industries leave the Caribbean almost uniformly with a severe unemployment problem. The lowest rate of overt unemployment in the region outside of Cuba is Trinidad and Tobago's—13.4 percent in 1977. The highest is thought to be in Haiti, where the United Nations in 1972 estimated urban unemployment and underemployment combined at about 50 percent. That the unemployment trend has been worsening is clear from these percentages:

Puerto Rico	1968	11.1	1977	19.9
Barbados	1960	11.3	1977	16.3
Jamaica	1960	13.0	1977	24.2

Exceptions to the trend are only temporary. And, in Cuba, full employment has been obtained at the expense of productivity, so that the rate of underemployment—unemployment in disguise—is quite high.

Without fundamental changes in contemporary Caribbean economies, the future will be even grimmer. The proportions of

Tourism is Barbados' largest foreign exchange earner

the adult populations who were economically active in 1970 in the main countries of the region ranged from 31 percent for Cuba, Jamaica and Trinidad, down to 25 percent for Puerto Rico compared with 44.5 percent for the United States in the same year. If we consider the rates at which these populations are growing, the dimensions of the problem become overwhelming. The annual rate of population increase in the United States in 1980, excluding migration, was 0.7 percent. By contrast, the aggregate rate in 1980 for Cuba, the Dominican Republic, Haiti, Jamaica, Trinidad and Tobago, and Puerto Rico—containing nearly 90 percent of the region's population—was over 2 percent. The Dominican Republic, at 3.1 percent, has the highest population growth rate of any country in the region, equivalent to a doubling of its population in only 23 years.

The Region's Economy: Performance and Prospects

Is there enough economic growth in prospect for the Caribbean to absorb such a fast-growing labor force? If we look at the record of recent economic performance, the picture is mixed but offers no ground for complacency about the future. In sugar, the region's traditional staple, the Caribbean share of world produc-

37

Table 3

Some Major Sources of Income

Countries	Production of sugar and bauxite in 1977 as a percent of production in 1968		Tourist receipts in 1977 as a percent of tourist receipts in 1974	Total per capita aid disbursed in U.S. dollars[a]
	Sugar	Bauxite		
Antigua	0	—	—	—
Bahamas	0	—	113	2.86
Barbados	71	—	109	25.60
Belize	151	—	—	71.43
Bermuda	—	—	159	0.50
Cuba	131	—	—	3.39[b]
Dominican Republic	189	57	172	6.67
French Guiana	—	—	—	1,086.66
Grenada	—	—	100	—
Guadeloupe	57	—	—	443.06
Guyana	75	91	75	14.74
Haiti	81	163	195	15.67
Jamaica	64	136	80	14.17
Martinique	38	—	—	512.16
Netherlands An-tilles	—	—	108	176.25
Puerto Rico	41	—	116	—
St. Kitts-Nevis-An-guilla	116	—	—	—
Suriname	59	86	143	186.59
Trinidad and To-bago	71	—	132	4.77
Caribbean, Total	118	109	115	—
World, Total	137	170	138	—

[a]Includes only disbursements of bilateral official development assistance from developed market economies and disbursements from multilateral institutions. These are 1975-77 annual averages.
[b]Excludes Soviet or Eastern European aid.

Source: *UN Statistical Yearbook* (1978)

tion fell all through the 1970s; only the Dominican Republic, Belize and, less consistently, Cuba increased their output. In bauxite, the Caribbean share of world production fell by almost half in the same years; no Caribbean bauxite-producing country kept up with the world growth rate (see Table 3, p. 38). A smaller drop also appeared in the region's share of global tourist receipts. Per capita agricultural production in the 1960s and 1970s fell in Jamaica, Guyana, Haiti, and Trinidad and Tobago. These difficulties have been made worse by the oil price rises that began in the early 1970s, as a result of which most countries of the region—with the conspicuous exception of oil-exporting Trinidad and Tobago—have experienced sustained deficits in their current-account payments balances and have consequently incurred heavy foreign debts.

Some countries, it is true, have done better than before, partly through the industrial diversification already described. Among the countries that increased their real per capita GDP from 1960 to 1979 were the Dominican Republic, Haiti, Guyana, Trinidad and Tobago, Barbados, Jamaica and the Bahamas. But after all, *some* growth over a 20-year period is a very limited standard of achievement—especially for the poorest countries and those that tolerate the widest economic inequality. Haiti is still one of the poorest countries in the world, where four-fifths of the children under age five suffer from protein-calorie malnutrition, with 17 percent classified as severely malnourished. In the Dominican Republic, despite its considerable economic growth, the corresponding rates are 75 percent malnourished, 4 percent severely. In more-egalitarian societies such as Guyana and Jamaica, despite their severe economic difficulties, the performance in regard to nutrition is highly creditable.

These trends suggest how difficult it is to achieve economic growth along with a real improvement in the standards of living of most people—not just the rich few—in small countries with limited resources and a heritage of slavery. Allowing for these handicaps, most have done well indeed, but not well enough to meet the needs of their fast-growing and underemployed populations—or to fulfill the dreams of their poets and politicians.

The Search for a Development Model

No Caribbean country has eschewed economic growth as an objective—nor, at the other extreme, has any Caribbean country stated that it is not interested in improving the distribution of income. Few if any, however, have substantially realized both goals. The Dominican Republic, notable for sheer gross national product (GNP) growth, has severe problems of poverty and social inequity. Cuba, whose central planning and state ownership of most means of production have brought about a tolerably equitable sharing of scarcities, has suffered periodic economic collapses and compiled an unimpressive economic growth record in the two decades since its revolution, despite continued heavy dependence on Soviet aid. Any country of the region seeking a strategy that would combine growth and social equity would have difficulty finding a model among its regional neighbors.

An arguable exception is Barbados, which has made a record of solid economic growth, low to moderate inflation and a reasonably good social performance; moreover it has maintained its brand of competitive politics, in which parties and politicians rotate in office. The Barbadian strategy, however, has resulted in some worsening of income distribution. It has also meant a very heavy dependence on the United Kingdom and on the United States in trade, investment, tourism and migration, and in cultural norms as well. Aside from its social cost, the example of Barbados holds little appeal for nationalist sentiment and has not been widely emulated.

The example that has perhaps been most influential is that of Puerto Rico—although few are willing to admit this because Puerto Rico is not independent. Several elements of Puerto Rico's approach to development have been adopted to one degree or another elsewhere in the region. For example, such countries as the Dominican Republic and Barbados, in order to diversify their economies and reduce dependence on agricultural and raw material production, have emulated Puerto Rico in offering tax and financial incentives to attract foreign private direct investment in the manufacturing and tourist sectors. In fact, industrialization by invitation, as it has been called, has played some role in most countries of the region; in many cases the enterprise is limited to final assembly of parts made elsewhere. In some cases this approach has produced impressive economic growth rates; but it has not always been accompanied, as it was in Puerto Rico, by better distribution of income.

A second way in which the Puerto Rican model has been influential is in the important economic role of government. Beginning in the 1940s and continuing to some degree ever since, the Puerto Rican government created a mixed public-private economy. Side by side with foreign investment, it created and administered state enterprises; it also acted to ensure that the benefits of growth would be shared more widely. A similar, but more single-minded, emphasis on the role of government later appeared in Jamaica under Michael Manley and in Guyana under Forbes Burnham. Both of these chief executives believed that by enlarging the role of the state, but stopping short of what had been done in Cuba, they might gain some of the distributional benefits achieved in Cuba, and also reduce their countries' dependence on foreign firms—but without sacrificing economic growth. Their governments took control of many foreign firms to achieve these ends. Their strategies have not had much success; economic growth rates have been low and at times negative, and the gains in improved distribution and in independence from foreign control have not been sufficient to justify the economies' poor performance.

A third feature of the Puerto Rican experience, for many years, was the export of people to the metropolitan power. Virtually all Caribbean countries have taken this path, too—including Cuba, exporting its political as well as its economic discontent to the United States. Like Puerto Rico, most of these countries have severe problems with unemployment when international migration, for one reason or another, drops off. In fact, the attractiveness of Puerto Rico as a model was brought into question in the 1970s, in part because its underemployment and unemployment rates became so high.

A final feature of the Puerto Rican model has been "foreign aid." In the case of Puerto Rico, the aid was not, strictly speaking, foreign. Massive transfers from the U.S. Federal government have been essential to keep Puerto Rico's economy afloat. Over half the population of Puerto Rico receives some form of U.S. Federal aid—food stamps, aid to dependent children, or welfare. As is evident from Table 3, massive foreign aid inflows characterize most Caribbean countries—including Cuba, unique though it is in many other respects. The U.S.S.R. pays prices well above world prices for Cuban sugar and nickel; it also provides balance-of-payments assistance, aid for specific development projects, and weaponry free of charge.

Dependence: An Enduring Reality

Successful or not in economic and social terms, the economic policies and expedients which the Caribbean states have variously tried all seem to point to one constant reality: their dependence on stronger powers outside the region. The same truth emerges from the nature of the borrowings from the Puerto Rican model—incentives to foreign investors, emigration of the jobless poor, acceptance of foreign aid in one form or another, and dependence on one or two countries for most of their foreign trade (see Table 2).

Foreign aid to the region, in fact, has been rapidly on the rise: excluding Cuba and the territories under foreign sovereignty, the annual aid flow from all non-Communist sources rose from $220 million in 1977 to $610 million in 1979. Much of the aid, in turn, being in the form of loans, creates another form of dependence— indebtedness. In 1978 Guyana and Jamaica were paying out a fifth or more of their export earnings in debt service, a situation that led in Jamaica to much bitterness between the government of former Prime Minister Manley and the International Monetary Fund. Cuba is massively indebted to the Soviet Union. It benefited in the early 1970s from a Soviet decision to postpone further Cuban debt payments until the second half of the 1980s, and more recently from a Soviet policy of increased trade subsidies to keep new debts from accumulating. In the whole region, only three countries have been relatively free of debt problems: Trinidad and Tobago with its oil; Barbados with its well-managed economy; and Haiti, whose stagnant economy, at least until the early 1970s, could attract few lenders.

Thus the constraints of the Caribbean's history, geography and economic structure continue to weigh heavily on its economic prospects. Strategies that aim simply to increase economic growth have been surprisingly successful, although perhaps only for a time and at significant social expense. But no country has managed to combine growth with equity, employment and greater economic independence. Instead, these values have repeatedly proved mutually incompatible, and strategies aimed at such multiple goals remain disappointing and troublesome. The search for a better development strategy in the Caribbean, then, remains open.

Is Regional Integration the Answer?

For the past quarter-century, many Caribbean leaders have argued that the solution to these dilemmas is regional integration. Some form of political and/or economic integration, it is thought, might minimize the disadvantages of small size and reduce the region's marked dependence on more-industrialized countries. The West Indies Federation, the Caribbean Free Trade Association, and the Caribbean Community and Common Market (CARICOM, created in 1973, consisting of 12 English-speaking Caribbean states) were all created in an attempt to realize these goals of regional integration. But the first two organizations are dead and CARICOM is in serious trouble. One major Trinidadian newspaper recently argued that "CARICOM deserves a decent burial."

The problems of all these bodies have been numerous, and their achievements, though real, quite limited. The poorer countries complain that CARICOM encourages economic growth in the already more-developed countries of the region, which become poles of growth while the less-developed become poles of stagnation. In general, there is little evidence that these bodies have lessened the English-speaking Caribbean countries' economic dependence.

No regional integration plan in the Caribbean has ever

included all the countries of the region. Part of the explanation may lie in the region's colonial history and in its linguistic and cultural fragmentation, but another obstacle arises from the different approaches to development. To allow Haiti, for example, to become a member might appear to Jamaica or Trinidad and Tobago to be more detrimental than beneficial. For Haiti itself, the prospect of becoming even more of a pole of stagnation after joining might not be appealing.

Nonetheless, there is good reason to continue to pursue well-designed cooperation projects among countries of the Caribbean where these can enable small national economies to complement one another and achieve economies of scale. Significantly, aid for regional cooperation is one of the aims of the Caribbean Group for Cooperation in Economic Development, a consortium of 31 aid-giving and aid-receiving governments and 16 financial institutions brought together in 1977 by the United States and the World Bank to coordinate foreign economic assistance to all countries of the region except Cuba. And a substantial share of the U.S. economic assistance proposed for the Caribbean in fiscal 1981 was earmarked for regional cooperation projects.

It would be unfortunate if the Caribbean countries were to abandon too soon the strategy of regional integration. It is possible that the specific regional integration plans tried thus far are at fault, and that a different approach could achieve more success. On the other hand, the experience of the last quarter-century clearly points to severe structural, historical and geographical constraints that regional integration alone, no matter how well designed, could probably never totally transcend.

This is, in sum, the trademark of Caribbean countries. Their governments continue to try strategy after strategy rather than surrender to the dependency and underdevelopment that is their legacy. To what extent they may ultimately succeed will depend partly on their own policies and partly on those of the United States and other powers outside this region—a subject to which we return in the final chapter.

4

Caribbean Politics: Stability, Violence and the Currencies of Power

Caribbean politics may face a crucial turning point in the early 1980s. To understand its significance, we should first note the region's high degree of political stability in the recent past. From the mid-1960s until 1979, when the governments of Grenada and Suriname were toppled, no Caribbean government was overthrown by force. This is a record not matched by any other region of the world outside of North America during those years. Yet the political stability of the Caribbean in the recent past has been largely based on three conditions: insularity, dependence and a tradition of charismatic leadership. Of these only the first seems likely to endure unchanged.

Insularity as a Stabilizing Factor

The stabilizing effect of insularity arises from an obvious fact of geography. Except for the Guianas and Belize on the mainland, and for Haiti and the Dominican Republic which share a single island, all the states of the region are bounded by salt water; thus their boundaries are easy to define and to defend.

None needs to maintain a substantial military force to protect its territorial integrity against regional neighbors. Not surprisingly, the few military coups in the Caribbean have occurred either in the larger countries—Cuba, Haiti and the Dominican Republic—which have always had substantial military forces, or on the South American mainland, as in Suriname, which has had boundary disputes with its neighbors and maintains a small army. The coup there in 1980 grew out of a wage dispute between soldiers and the government.

Even the small island states, to be sure, have the problem of controlling their armed forces, though the problem has generally proved manageable. Outside of Cuba, there are no armed forces in the Caribbean that are truly professional—highly trained in modern warfare, disciplined, led by a skilled officer corps, proud of their military institutions and reliably responsive to the chain of command. Armed forces elsewhere serve primarily as a police force to quell civil disturbances. Being unprofessional, they cannot claim—as some South American officer corps have done—that they would rule more effectively than civilians. Military personnel are often co-opted by civilian rulers to share in the spoils of ruling. Thus the armed forces obtain many of the benefits of political power without the trouble of seizing it. Stability is thus maintained, but at a public cost.

Even in countries where coups have occurred in times past, there have been fewer in recent years. In Haiti, for example, President François Duvalier developed a quasi-monarchical procedure for political succession and upon his death, power passed peacefully to his son. While the Dominican Republic had a chaotic political experience in the mid-1960s, its longer-term experience has been marked first by incumbent control under the long dictatorship of Trujillo, then, since the late 1960s, by a constitutional system that has even transferred power through free elections (admittedly with an assist from the U.S. government to make certain that the election results were observed) from one government party to its opposition. And in Cuba there has been no military coup since the revolution led by Castro which put him in power.

Dependence as a Force for Stability

Dependence on outside powers is sure to remain an important force for stability in the region, but it may be less potent than it was. Until the early 1960s much of the Caribbean's stability could be explained simply by the fact that colonial powers kept order in their colonies. This is still the case in the surviving U.S., British, French and Dutch dependencies, where dependence often extends even to habits of thought and behavior. In Martinique, for example, the poet Aimé Césaire, even while championing the proud doctrine of *négritude* for his fellow blacks, has looked to France for his literary models and has held office under the French system.

Real dependence does not, of course, necessarily end with the coming of formal independence. Political stability in both colonies and independent countries has been bolstered by the export of people—political troublemakers and the underemployed—to the United States and Europe, a process allowed and reinforced by dependence. Earlier chapters have discussed the support of the Cuban revolution by massive Soviet aid; Cuba has also borrowed extensively from Soviet economic and political institutions, ideology and practice. Heavy dependence on the former colonial power has been noted in the quite different case of Barbados. It is reasonable to expect that the process of formal decolonization in the region, now nearing completion, will gradually lessen the influence of the former colonial powers. This trend may well make the Caribbean more unstable politically than it has been in the recent past.

Charisma as a Force for Stability

A third source of political stability in the Caribbean has been the prevalence of charismatic leadership linked to a mass movement. But this phenomenon, too, may be less important in the future.

Charisma may be defined as that quality that makes the people believe that its possessor is endowed with special graces, whether divine or secular and historical, that empower him to rule over them; the leader, in turn, believes in his own special right to rule.

In the Caribbean, charismatic leaders have dominated the recent political life of several major countries. Castro in Cuba, Williams in Trinidad and Tobago, Alexander Bustamante in Jamaica and Muñoz Marín in Puerto Rico have all had this quality. Charismatic leaders typically emerge at times of crisis, such as the approach of independence or the emergence of a revolution—situations that were frequent in the Caribbean in the 1950s.

Even a highly magnetic politician cannot long succeed without organizing ability. Most of the Caribbean's charismatic politicians have built up impressive political organizations, such as Puerto Rico's Popular Democratic party, Trinidad and Tobago's People's National Movement, or Cuba's Communist party. Significantly, the only head of government in the English-speaking Caribbean to have been overthrown, Eric Gairy of Grenada, had shown, under colonial rule as well as subsequently, that he lacked the ability to be more than "a hero to the crowd" because he could not build an effective political party.

One-man rule, in fact, is common in countries that have just been through the drama of independence or revolution. Whether or not the leader possesses charismatic qualities, the political system centers overwhelmingly on him and he tends to rely on his personal strengths and to trust only close relatives and associates. In a very small country, most of the nation's elite families may also be included in the political power structure.

Kinship also serves in such a system as an important means of organizing political succession—contributing further to political stability. The laws of revolutionary Cuba provide that Fidel Castro should be succeeded by his brother Raúl in the event of Fidel's death. Two Manleys have served as prime ministers of Jamaica. The current prime minister of Barbados, "Tom" Adams, is the son of the former prime minister of the ill-fated West Indies Federation. The Duvaliers, father and son, have ruled Haiti for over two decades.

In general, however, the dominance of charismatic leaders poses a serious problem for political stability in the long run because of their frequent inability to transfer power except by dying. Thus Williams and Castro, two long-lived political leaders with quite different styles, have both been unwilling or unable to arrange for political succession during their own lifetimes. The only one of the Caribbean's major political figures of the recent past to have done so was the late Governor Muñoz Marín of Puerto Rico.

Charismatic and highly personalized leadership, then, although a long-standing source of political order in the Caribbean, has instability built into it. As the heroic deeds become history, as the leaders age and die, and as the movements lose their political glitter, stability becomes problematic. The charismatic tradition, moreover, may make the attainment of stability by other means much less likely. People may have become so accustomed to relying on single powerful leaders, or on a few families, that it is more difficult for them to conceive of other bases of legitimate rule. This is one reason why, in the early 1980s, the impressive political order of the Caribbean's past 15 years may come to an end.

If this should prove true, one unhappy result could be a wider occurrence of the violence that has been a part of normal politics for many years, especially in Haiti and the Dominican Republic. Already the sharpened electoral competition in Jamaica has led political parties and movements to use violence against their opponents. Violence, too, has been used over the years in Guyana's politics as a means of competition and intimidation. Violence reappeared briefly in Cuba in 1980, aimed against some of those leaving the country, organized in part by local "committees for the defense of the revolution." Violence has been a trademark of one wing of the independence movement in Puerto Rico. The coexistence of governmental stability and competitive political violence has rendered these political systems fragile without, until now, necessarily making them less durable.

High Stakes: The Currencies of Political Power

To deal with weak economies and precarious politics, most Caribbean regimes have undertaken a great many tasks, making the people more and more dependent on government and further centralizing political power. A highly articulated political rheto-

49

ric underlies a consensus among politicians in the region that the state should intervene in the economy and society. The result, however, may be greater political vulnerability, since citizens increasingly hold government responsible for various aspects of social and economic life. Thus the stakes of politics rise.

The sources and uses of this state power are varied. In the Caribbean's most powerful state, Cuba, power derives from the revolution and from Castro's leadership. It has been used to achieve many praiseworthy aims in such fields as education and public health, but it has also been abused to curtail civil liberties and to maintain a very high degree of political authoritarianism. Although no other Caribbean state—for good or ill—is as strong as Cuba, many others have surprising powers and responsibilities. For example, although Puerto Rican economic development owes much to the private sector and to investments from the U.S. mainland, another essential ingredient was the rise of affiliated state enterprises during the 1940s. These have continued to grow ever since. Another Caribbean country known for its openness to private enterprise, the Dominican Republic, also has a large public sector derived from the confiscation of the vast personal holdings of the late dictator Trujillo. In the English-speaking Caribbean, the source of state power—and of the state's relative immunity to popular pressure—is primarily the bureaucracy, with habits of thought and practice little changed since the colonial era.

The strength of the state, in fact, inevitably means the strength of the bureaucracy. All through Caribbean politics can be seen the coexistence of strong bureaucratic organizations with charismatic political leaders. Political leaders can often impose their will on the bureaucracy, as Castro has done in Cuba. But even in Cuba, and certainly elsewhere, the bureaucracy has impressive powers of its own.

Contenders in the political arena, then, may use various currencies of power, one being appeals to and interventions by the "great" leader, and another being organizational or bureaucratic power. Another currency of power emerges from formal or informal dependence on a stronger country. Defeated political groups can appeal to the past or present colonial power, or to a stronger neighbor, to redress the political imbalance in their favor. The Soviet Union sought to change the policies and personnel of the Cuban government in 1968. The United States and Britain contributed to a change of government in Guyana prior to independence in 1966. External powers may also act to bolster incumbents, as the United States and Venezuela did in assisting Williams to overcome internal disturbances in Trinidad and Tobago in 1970, or as Barbados did in helping St. Vincent-Grenadines almost ten years later to reconquer Union Island, occupied by some followers of the Rastafarian movement (a Messianic and apocalyptic cult). British and Dutch interventions are likely to be less frequent, however, as their remaining colonies become independent.

A fourth currency of power is electoral strength. Elections have played an essential role in the politics of the entire Caribbean except for Haiti and Cuba. Even in Cuba, local elections have increased the influence of citizens on local government. Incumbent governments have actually been defeated at the polls and replaced by the opposition in Barbados, St. Lucia, Dominica, Jamaica, the Dominican Republic, and repeatedly in Puerto Rico.

Some currencies of power are quite informal. In very small countries, citizens are accustomed to making personal contacts with political leaders and bureaucracies, offering political support in return for favors for themselves, their families and their neighborhoods.

To gain favors from a bureaucratized state, however, requires not just personal connections but also organized interest groups. Government, in turn, often chooses to sponsor interest groups, pre-empting political space in order to prevent the emergence of politically uncontrolled lobbies. This has happened in Cuba, with its mass organizations under the "guidance" of the Communist party, and in the Dominican Republic, with its "corporate" tradition of government-chartered organizations. It also happened in the English-speaking Caribbean under British rule, when the Labor government of the 1940s reversed an earlier opposition to the spread of labor unions in the region and began to promote the unions' links to local Labor parties—the aim being to foster an eventual social-democratic political order. Jamaican governments have also promoted, subsidized and, to some degree, controlled such varied organizations as the Jamaican Agricultural Society, the All-Island Cane Farmers Association, the All-Island Banana Growers Association, and the Citrus Growers Association.

Two stabilizing factors of the past cannot be counted on for the future: the colonial system is nearly gone and the outstanding leaders of the independence generation will soon be growing old. The many responsibilities states have assumed give rise to large political claims, on which neither the politicians nor the governments and movements they claim to lead have enough resources to deliver. Bold assertions of independence can be found side by side with the inescapable fact of continued dependence on, and in some countries fascination with, the former or present colonial powers. Many of these political contradictions have been contained by the region's apparent political stability. If that is further weakened beyond the somewhat aberrant cases of Grenada and Suriname—as recurrent political violence in several countries suggests it may be—the Caribbean's political landscape may be permanently changed in the 1980s.

5

Emigration:
The Caribbean Diaspora

Perhaps nothing better illustrates the dependent position of the Caribbean through five centuries than the mass movement of laborers into, within, and out of the region. In an earlier era, European industrial capital, short of cheap labor for the mines and plantations in the Caribbean colonies of exploitation, imported millions of slaves and indentured workers to fill the need. Today, the capital that is short of cheap labor is not in the Caribbean but in North America and Europe—while much of the labor surplus is in the Caribbean. The terms of the transaction, however, have not changed fundamentally, even though the extreme inhumanity of plantation slavery is mercifully past. No less than before, the Caribbean people who migrate to work in the industrial economies—where native workers generally resent them as low-wage competitors—come not entirely of their own volition but are driven by necessity. No less than their ancestors, the members of this Caribbean diaspora are pawns of industrial capital, participants in what is now a nearly worldwide process of international labor migration. Caribbean communities in the United States, Canada and

Western Europe, for all but a fortunate few, are not colonies of exploitation but colonies of the exploited.

The migratory process, in fact, has been continuous through the centuries, both within and beyond the Caribbean. In times of slavery, planters and brokers bought and sold slaves within the region almost as much as in transatlantic trade. Whatever attachment Caribbean people developed to their islands of birth, it was traditionally superseded by the necessities of work.

When slavery ended, the patterns of labor migration did not change to any great extent. As late as 1870, Barbadian planters were encouraging the working population of the island to leave for other sugar colonies in order to minimize frustration and violence among the unemployed. A view of emigration as an escape valve and immigration as a source of labor thus came to be established quite early in the Caribbean.

Enterprises other than sugar attracted British West Indian workers. Jamaicans, for the most part, constructed the first railroad across the isthmus of Panama (1848-55). Islanders from the Eastern Caribbean followed in 1880 to work for the Universal Inter-Oceanic Canal Company in Panama; after the failure of this company in the late 1880s many worked on sugar and banana plantations in Central America. The largest wave of West Indian migrants to Central America, an estimated 100,000, came in the first years of the 20th century to work mainly for the United Fruit Company or the Panama Canal Company. With the completion of the canal in 1914, some 10,000 West Indians from Curaçao, Trinidad and Barbados found work in the new oil fields of Venezuela. By 1923, Curaçao with its oil refineries had itself become a magnet for labor. And between 1910 and 1930 thousands of Jamaican workers moved to Cuba.

West Indian Emigration from the Caribbean

It was also in the second and third decades of the 20th century that significant numbers of British West Indians first emigrated to the United States. About 46,000 arrived during those years. This migration inspired a cultural renaissance that is still remembered in New York's Harlem, and led hundreds of thousands of British West Indians to migrate to the United States in later decades.

The heaviest emigration of Caribbeans to North America and Europe followed World War II. British West Indian workers were imported into Britain during the war and were recruited in large numbers in the immediate postwar period. By 1968 there were 320,000 British West Indians in Britain; 150,000 (mostly French) West Indians had found their way under similar circumstances to France; and some 20,000 from the Dutch colonies had migrated to the Netherlands. A relaxation of U.S. immigration policies during World War II saw the entry of substantial numbers of British West Indians into the United States in the 1940s, still more in the 1950s, and almost half a million in the 1960s. When the final tally for the 1970s is made, it may well exceed half a million.

But the movements of British West Indians followed as much from the closing as from the opening of borders. Laws designed to exclude black people were enacted toward the end of the 1920s in most Central American republics. Cuba followed suit in the 1930s. In 1929, Venezuela began to restrict the entry of foreign-born blacks, and in 1931 most British West Indian workers were sent home from Curaçao.

A generation later, doors were closing in Europe and North America. The Commonwealth Immigration Act of 1962 curtailed the flow of British West Indians to the United Kingdom, following a two-and-a-half year period in which 168,000 West Indians had entered the country. British policy became even more restrictive in 1965, when a White Paper was issued stating that black people were a problem for the United Kingdom and proposing to restrict immigration from regions of the Commonwealth in which blacks predominated. Canada has long since had an explicit bias against nonwhites in its immigration policy; in 1962 it substituted educational and occupational requirements whose practical effect was much the same.

U.S. immigration policies, although more subtle, have had similar effects in the last half-century. The U.S. Immigration and Nationality Act of 1952 (the McCarran-Walter Act), like earlier laws going back to the 1920s, exempted from national quotas those Western Hemisphere nations that were independent at the time of its enactment. Since most of the Caribbean islands were then still colonies, legal immigration to the United States from these islands was severely curtailed. Further impediments were added in 1965 when labor certification requirements were imposed and when quotas were applied for the first time to immigration from countries of the Western Hemisphere. The limit at first was a simple hemisphere-wide quota of 120,000 a year, with no ceilings for individual countries. In 1976, however, Congress decided to apply to the Western Hemisphere country limits that had been in effect for the rest of the world since 1965. Congress also extended a perference system to the Western Hemisphere which facilitated the entry of close relatives of U.S. residents but severely curtailed the immigration of West Indians as skilled or unskilled workers.

As doors have closed, British West Indians have turned to new countries of employment—or to new ways of gaining employment in the same countries. Many British West Indians have entered the United States in the last 15 to 20 years with tourist visas, have then overstayed their visits, and obtained jobs as undocumented workers. A clue to the size of this illegal migration is the fact that from 1963 to 1973 the number of Barbadians, Trinidadians, Bermudians and St. Lucians admitted to the United States on *nonimmigrant* visas more than quadrupled; the number so admitted from the island of Dominica increased more than tenfold; and the number of Jamaicans, from 29,046 to 113,300. Some, but not many, are turned back: the number of Jamaicans required to depart the United States because of violations of their tourist visas jumped from 410 in 1963 to 1,557 in 1973.

It is estimated that there were some 50,000 Barbadians, close to half a million Jamaicans, and some 150,000 Trinidadians in the United States in 1980. Well over half live in the New York metropolitan area, with smaller communities in southern Florida and in many large cities of the Northeast. Occupationally and educationally they are much more diverse than most recent migrant communities. Of the legal migrants, between 5 percent and 10 percent are highly educated professionals—roughly the same proportion as among recent European immigrants. On the other hand, since 1967 a large number of the immigrant visas issued to Barbadians, Jamaicans, and Trinidadians have gone to women employed as private household workers, and for years there has been a persistent flow of West Indian contract agricultural workers into rural Florida, New Jersey and New England. Skilled and semiskilled workers are thought to make up the bulk of the illegal population.

For both the United States and the Caribbean, British West Indian migration poses some difficult problems. Helped by the high quality of West Indian schools and qualified for a wide variety of occupations, British West Indians in this country have higher incomes and more prestigious jobs than Afro-Americans (though by no means as high as white Americans). U.S. employers apparently prefer to hire West Indians over native blacks either because they are better educated and trained or, in the case of illegals, because, being more vulnerable, they accept lower wages and demand fewer benefits. As a result, there is a fair amount of resentment in the Afro-American community toward the West Indian newcomers.

For West Indian societies, on the other hand, emigration points up once again the realities of dependence arising from inadequate development. Emigration relieves population density, alleviates unemployment and provides income in the form of remittances from those who left home. On the other hand, it drains these countries of their most skilled personnel, whom they had the burden of educating. The high-quality schools available in the West Indies could yet become an ingredient in making island economies thrive—if other essential ingredients such as capital and assured markets were present on a sufficient scale. As it is, education has combined with rapid population growth to give these societies a skilled working class and an able professional class far larger than their limping economies can absorb. Thus emigration has become the "Catch-22" of West Indian dependence: without it the region's economies would be a shambles; with it, they are losing much of the skill and talent that could, under other conditions, lift them into durable prosperity.

Puerto Rican Migration to the Mainland

In the case of Puerto Rico, emigration has responded mainly to U.S. industrial labor needs. Puerto Ricans won the right to move at will to and from the mainland in 1917 when they were granted U.S. citizenship, but few exercised this right until World War II, when a serious increase in unemployment on the island and a labor shortage on the mainland led to massive recruitment of poorer Puerto Ricans to man mainland industries. When wartime travel restrictions were lifted, more tens of thousands of Puerto Ricans hurried aboard inexpensive flights in response to postwar industries' demand for cheap labor. It was the first airborne migration in history.

Between 1950 and 1960, the number of persons of Puerto Rican birth in New York alone rose by 292,000. Of these early migrants, most were men between 15 and 45, although many were young women and children. All were predominantly lower-class and rural or semirural in origin. Many were black or racially mixed. It was these characteristics of the early postwar migrants that set the Anglo-American stereotype of Puerto Ricans and the ways in which new arrivals from the island would be incorporated into mainland society. Puerto Ricans settled heavily in the New York metropolitan area. There and elsewhere, their numbers grew quickly as mortality rates decreased and a second generation was born. By 1980, this population easily exceeded 2 million, or about 40 percent of all Puerto Ricans in the world. However, changes in the economy in the last 15 years and the expansion of social welfare programs on the island have greatly diminished the flow of Puerto Ricans to the mainland. In fact, in recent years the net movement has been back to Puerto Rico.

As second- and third-generation Puerto Ricans increase in numbers on the mainland, an uneasy relationship—familiar to many other immigrant nationality groups in America—has emerged between island Puerto Rican society and its mainland

A bilingual school in the Bronx, New York

The Christian Science Monitor

counterpart. Although New York Puerto Ricans identify themselves strongly as Puerto Rican in the context of ethnic relations in New York, they increasingly find themselves strangers to the language, values and lifestyles of island Puerto Ricans. For their part, island Puerto Ricans—although they continue to regard U.S. treatment of mainland Puerto Ricans as a personal affront—find these emigrants so foreign to the island society that they have coined for them a derogatory term, "Neo Ricans." Thus, dependency has created new divisions among Puerto Ricans.

The Dominican Migrants

Migration from the Dominican Republic to the United States is far newer than either the West Indian or Puerto Rican migrations; yet the underlying forces in all three cases are quite similar. There was little Dominican emigration until the mid-1960s. Then, in a movement unprecedented in Dominican history, an estimated 400,000 Dominicans—about 8 percent of the country's population—moved to the United States in a period of 15 years. To evade U.S. immigration restrictions, a large proportion of these entered the country with fraudulent documents, or overstayed their tourist visas.

Traditional wisdom associates this massive Dominican emigration with the political turmoil that followed the fall of Trujillo in 1961. But the fact that the flow became much heavier in the late 1960s and early 1970s suggests that Dominicans, like British West Indians and Puerto Ricans, have emigrated primarily to find work. Displaced in large numbers by changes in capital investment in the Dominican economy, they too responded to the attraction of the North American labor market. Ironically, this period of heaviest emigration of Dominicans was also the period of greatest economic growth—unfortunately capital-intensive and poorly distributed—in the country they left behind.

Dominican migrants to the United States are less well educated than British West Indian migrants, though more so than the first waves of Puerto Rican migrants to the mainland. A large number come from the north central region of the country known as the Cibao, often called the Dominican food basket, where many owned land or small businesses. More and more of them appear to be in a class above the destitute, if not quite part of the entrepreneurial middle class. In the New York area, where most have settled, they live in heavily Hispanic neighborhoods, take many of the same jobs in the service and textile industries open to other new immigrant groups, and often pass for Puerto Rican to prevent problems with immigration officials. The fact that some 40 percent have returned at least once to the Dominican Republic suggests that they, too, are not destitute in New York.

Emigration from Haiti and Cuba

Haitian and Cuban migrants to the United States are not much different in economic and social terms from other Caribbean migrants, but in both these countries emigration in recent years has also had political origins.

In the case of Haiti, there is a long history of migration to, or temporary sojourns in, other countries. Working-class Haitians have served through most of this century as contract laborers in the Dominican Republic, cutting sugarcane at harvest time. Some Haitians became agricultural workers in the eastern provinces of Cuba in the 1930s. Sons of the small middle and upper classes of Haiti have traditionally attended schools in France.

The United States did not become a main destination for Haitian migrants until very recent years, despite Haiti's unlimited immigration rights (until 1976) under U.S. law. When François Duvalier came to power in 1957, his most prominent opponents—a small number of the Haitian elite—found their way to this country as quasi-political refugees. Then in the mid-1960s, as unemployment in Haiti rose sharply and Duvalier tightened his dictatorship, declaring himself President for Life, there was a mass exodus of the lower middle class and, increasingly, of the urban working class.

Conditions in this country led many of this new wave of Haitians to claim the status of political refugees. The U.S. government responded by granting thousands the right to work in the United States without immigrant visas. Under this procedure the Haitian community of New York in the early and mid-1970s grew to over 300,000—three times the number of Haitians in the United States with official immigrant status.

It is difficult at best, in analyzing the Haitian emigration, to distinguish the economic from the political. The U.S. Immigration and Naturalization Service, as a practical matter, seems to have concluded in the Haitian case that people of low educational background cannot be classed as political refugees. Thus the boat people—perhaps as many as 30,000 who crossed the Caribbean from Haiti to Florida from 1972 to 1980—being mostly rural in origin, illiterate and only semiskilled, have been treated simply as illegal migrants from an underdeveloped economy. Like many undocumented migrants from other Caribbean countries, they find jobs in agro-industry, textiles and the service sector. The U.S. government, evidently undecided as to how or whether to legalize their status, has thus far left them in a legal and procedural limbo.

Largest of all the recent Caribbean migrations is the exodus of nearly a million Cubans in the 22 years since the Cuban revolution. Although unique in many ways, its history shows changes quite similar to those of the smaller Haitian emigration.

After the departure of Batista's supporters, the first major wave of emigrants, which began in 1960, was clearly political—primarily members of the upper class and high-level managers of large national and foreign concerns. For most of these people—highly educated, professional and white—settlement in the United States meant a loss of status, but for some it became a new opportunity to invest capital untouched by the Cuban revolution. It is this early wave which set the North American stereotype of the Cuban exile in the United States.

Thereafter, as in the West Indian case, Cuban emigration became increasingly diversified and democratized. The airlift of the late 1960s, explicitly authorized by Castro, brought mainly middle-class students, children, and housewives. Boats and flights via third countries in the 1960s carried skilled and semiskilled workers. But the sea lift of 1980, also authorized by Castro, carried unprecedented numbers of colored and black Cubans, single young adult males, and members of the urban working class. Today, while over a quarter of all Cuban households in this country have incomes above $25,000, close to 20 percent are below poverty level.

Although the Cubans have been admitted into the United States as political refugees, economic factors seem to loom larger with each new wave. Rationing and austerity are cited more and more as reasons for leaving; threats of political imprisonment are cited less and less. Castro's periodic open-exit policies increasingly appear to be his peculiar solution to the same deep structural economic problems that plague the rest of the Caribbean.

Neighbors in Our Midst

Whatever its roots, the effects of massive emigration are enormous for the Caribbean countries. And, despite the obvious inequality of power and wealth, the industrial countries to which the migrants have moved will feel the effects increasingly. For the Caribbean, beyond the alleviation of unemployment and population density, emigration further deepens the inevitable interpenetration with industrial countries. For the industrial countries, it simply underlines the impossibility of disengagement from the Caribbean. For the latter, indeed, the primary consequence is the expansion of Caribbean societies beyond their national borders and the possibility, sometime in the future, of Caribbean societies' exerting political pressure on industrial countries, above all the United States, from within.

As this possibility is gradually realized, Caribbean communities on the U.S. mainland, like earlier immigrant communities, may cease to be colonies of the exploited, and may take their places among the many elements that make up the diverse society and polity of the United States. They may then be in a position to influence the U.S. government not only on their own account but also on behalf of their countries of origin. Before this stage can be reached, however, both the Caribbean immigrants and their well-established North American neighbors must travel a long road of mutual accommodation and acceptance, in which the policies of the U.S. government will play a crucial part.

6

The Caribbean and United States Policy

The involvement of the United States in the Caribbean is not a matter of choice but of necessity. It arises from enduring facts of geography and history which, in turn, have created significant U.S. interests in the region. These interests can be summed up as follows:

1. *Military security.* The Caribbean, as part of the southern border of the United States, is a potential avenue of attack on this country by any power strong enough to mount or threaten such an attack. In the present era the only conceivable source of a threat of this kind would be the Soviet Union.

2. *Seaborne commerce.* Through the Caribbean travels much of the international shipping of the United States, Western Europe and Japan, as well as of mainland Latin American countries and the Caribbean islands themselves. Some of this traffic moves within the Caribbean basin; some transits the Caribbean and the Panama Canal to move between the Atlantic and Pacific. Prominent among the cargoes carried are petroleum (from Venezuela and Mexico, as well as Caribbean countries) and strategic minerals. Any closure of the Caribbean sea-lanes would interrupt travel through the Panama Canal and would

probably be considered an act of aggression by, among others, Venezuela. Again, the only power that could in the near future threaten such action is the Soviet Union.

3. *Strategic imports.* In bauxite and its derivative, alumina, the Caribbean in 1978 accounted for 54 percent of U.S. imports, the great bulk coming from Jamaica and Suriname. Since the United States imports 90 percent of its requirements of these materials, this trade alone gives the Caribbean considerable strategic significance in the U.S. economy. In addition, about 8 percent of U.S. requirements of primary nickel are imported from the Dominican Republic. Nickel imports from Cuba, a former U.S. supplier and the main Caribbean nickel producer, are barred by the U.S. trade embargo.

In 1976 Caribbean exports to the United States were valued at $6.4 billion—more than five times the figure for 1970. Most of the increase came from the soaring price of imported crude oil and petroleum products from three countries, the Bahamas (a petroleum transshipment and refining center), the Netherlands Antilles, and Trinidad and Tobago, which, although a small percentage of total U.S. oil imports, nevertheless provide the U.S. with about 500,000 barrels of oil per day.

4. *Trade and investment.* The region's share of U.S. trade and investment, while not large by world standards, is significant. In 1976 the Caribbean accounted for 1.9 percent of U.S. exports and 5 percent of U.S. imports—the great bulk of the latter consisting of petroleum, with bauxite, alumina, nickel, sugar, cocoa, and fruits and vegetables making up most of the remainder.

The U.S. direct investment position in the Caribbean (excluding Puerto Rico) in 1979 came to about $4.7 billion, or 2.5 percent of the book value of all U.S. foreign direct investment in that year. Two billion dollars of that, however, was in the Bahamas alone. There was a considerable decline in U.S. direct investment in the region after the Cuban revolution, when all U.S. investments in Cuba were expropriated. Jamaica and Guyana, among others, have also reduced the weight of U.S. and other foreign firms in their economies in recent years; to what extent this trend will be reversed in Jamaica by the Seaga government remains to be seen. The existing U.S. investment position in the Caribbean, however, remains very important for these small economies.

5. *Migration.* Caribbean peoples are not only this country's international neighbors; they are also increasingly neighbors in our midst. To the extent that their numbers continue to increase rapidly, while their economies and political systems fail to meet their basic needs, more and more are likely to join their relatives and friends, by legal means or otherwise, in the United States. As natural U.S. population growth continues to slow down, Caribbean as well as Mexican migrants and their children will account for an increasing share of U.S. population growth at least for the balance of this century. The demographic impact of the Caribbean on the United States seems certain to become an increasing focus of U.S. policy toward the region in the coming years.

New Interests, Old Attitudes

As the above short list shows, U.S. interests in the Caribbean have greatly evolved in recent decades. Yet the traditional attitudes which have formed U.S. policy toward the region have changed very little. As a great power dealing with neighbors of vastly inferior power, the United States has alternated between long periods of neglect and short periods of acute concern at the highest levels—the latter usually caused by fear of the intrusion of another great power from the outside.

For more than a century the focus of this fear was on the European powers, barred by the Monroe Doctrine (and by the British navy) from attempting to transfer to themselves any of the former or remaining Spanish colonies in the Western Hemisphere. The United States went beyond this protective policy in the decade following 1898, the year of its brief and victorious war with Spain. It acquired new territorial and strategic interests within the region which further accentuated its sensitivity to intrusion by outside powers, and gave a new meaning to the Monroe Doctrine. In June 1940, with Hitler's Germany victorious over France, the United States, though not yet a belligerent, applied a "no transfer" principle to all Dutch, French and

Gunboat diplomacy: U.S. Marines land in Haiti in 1915

British colonies in the Caribbean area and, to prevent their falling under German influence, occupied several of these territories in agreement with the occupying power, returning them when the war ended in 1945.

A Central Issue: Relations with Cuba

Given this traditional U.S. emphasis on strategic considerations in the Caribbean, it was perhaps inevitable that fears of other major-power involvement in the region should be transferred after World War II to the Soviet Union. The dominance of this fear became all the stronger after revolutionary Cuba emerged as a Soviet ally and, in October 1962, after the Soviet Union emplaced on Cuban soil strategic weapons which would have improved its capabilities in a nuclear showdown with the United States. The world came closer to full-scale nuclear war at that time than ever before or since. The crisis was resolved when the Soviet Union withdrew the offensive weapons on the understanding that the United States would not invade Cuba.

U.S. policy-makers ever since have tended to perceive Cuba primarily as a Soviet surrogate, and hence to make containment of Cuban influence a keystone of U.S. Caribbean policy. It was this principle, for example, that underlay U.S. intervention against the Juan Bosch faction in the Dominican Republic in 1965. In addition, the steady dismantling of the European colonial system in the region since the early 1960s led to fears in the United States that the passing of the old regional order would leave a "vacuum" and open up new opportunities for Cuba and its Soviet patron.

In fact, however, since the 1960s Cuba's most conspicuous actions against perceived U.S. interests have occurred outside the Western Hemisphere. Militarily, its main activity has been in Africa, the only theater where Cuba has deployed large combat units outside its own borders. Diplomatically, its main focus has been at the global level, in the worldwide Nonaligned Movement and at the UN.

Within the Caribbean, Cuba's influence in recent years has been significant but far from predominant. On the positive side, early in the 1970s, despite the U.S.-led diplomatic boycott, Trinidad and Tobago, Jamaica, Guyana and Barbados took the lead in establishing diplomatic relations with Cuba. After the overthrow of the eccentric tyrant Gairy in Grenada in March 1979, Cuba became the main regional backer of the new left-wing government, headed by Prime Minister Bishop. It has provided economic aid and military advisers to Grenada, as well as to the Nicaraguan revolutionary government. It has also carried on large economic aid programs in Guyana and Jamaica, but in the latter, Cubans were accused of meddling in internal affairs.

Cuba's relations with Guyana deteriorated in 1980 because of disputes over fishing rights and, a more serious matter, Cuban ties to Prime Minister Burnham's political opposition. Relations with Jamaica worsened after the October 1980 electoral victory of Edward Seaga, who promptly asked for the recall of the Cuban ambassador.

Meanwhile, Cuba's reach in the Caribbean has been shortened by its own economic troubles. The severity of the 1980 recession—the third in Cuba since the 1959 revolution—was advertised to the world by the desperate exodus of 125,000 citizens who left by boat for Florida, and of others who left by air for other countries of Latin America. About a third of the Cuban Council of Ministers, and many lower-ranking officials, were replaced in 1979-80. Repressive practices, abandoned during the 1970s, reappeared: students and faculty were dismissed from the universities for lack of ideological "depth," and many Cubans about to leave the country were victimized by government-sponsored "committees for the defense of the revolution." Although the government is still militarily strong and popular enough to weather these storms—all the more so since part of the opposition has been exported—Cuba is scarcely the picture of a country that is likely to be either admired as a model, or feared as a threat, by most of its Caribbean island neighbors.

Nor can the Soviet Union itself currently pose a threat to the United States from Cuban territory, despite the public alarm in this country in 1979 over the asserted presence in Cuba of a Soviet combat brigade. In response to expressed U.S. misgivings at that time, the Soviet Union and the United States came to an understanding that the U.S.S.R. will not introduce combat troops into Cuba in the future. This pledge reinforces the understanding of 1962 barring Soviet offensive missiles from Cuba, and that of 1970 barring the Soviet navy from using Cuba as a strategic base.

Conceivably, the Soviet navy, alone or with help from Cuba, could pose a threat to free transit through the Caribbean sea-lanes, although it could not do so without more naval strength in the area than it is likely to have for some years to come. To prevent such a threat is obviously an important U.S. military responsibility. In view of the strategic relationship between the two nuclear superpowers, however, the maintenance of an array of U.S. military bases in the region is no longer militarily appropriate or useful. The defense of the sea-lanes will depend largely on the general state of the U.S.-Soviet bilateral relationship.

69

Toward an Effective U.S. Cuba Policy

If past U.S. policy can be taken as a guide, it is likely that the United States will continue to fear, and seek to counteract, the spread of Cuban influence in the Caribbean—limited though that influence appears to be today. Following the revolution in Grenada, the Carter Administration adopted a policy of modest military-training aid to those countries of the region requesting it, virtually regardless of ideology. Such assistance was proposed for fiscal year 1981 to Barbados, St. Vincent-Grenadines, St. Lucia and Dominica—all the English-speaking neighbors of Grenada—as well as to Guyana and Jamaica. As the then Assistant Secretary of State for Inter-American Affairs William G. Bowdler explained to the Senate Foreign Relations Committee: "We do not want Cuba to become the primary alternative by default."

Although military programs on this small scale may have their place as one form of counterbalance to Cuban influence, they cannot be an effective basis for U.S. policy in the Caribbean. Indeed, it is wrong to suppose that the Soviet Union, or Cuba as its ally, constitutes the principal threat to U.S. interests in the region—even more wrong to suppose that the sole means of countering that threat is diplomatic and military containment. On the contrary, the fundamental sources of insecurity throughout the Caribbean are internal—political, economic, social and demographic. From these, combined with the steady withdrawal of the old colonial powers, arise the regionwide insecurity and the massive migrations that pose the Caribbean's most substantial contemporary threat to U.S. interests. It would be futile to expect a Cuba locked into a posture of hostility toward the United States not to seek and find opportunities to exploit the resulting tensions, and no U.S. policy of containment can prevent it from doing so.

A more effective policy in the long run would be to negotiate at long last a renewal of U.S. diplomatic relations with Cuba, and to end the economically ineffective and diplomatically troublesome trade embargo. Efforts to accomplish this were undertaken briefly by the Ford Administration and again in the first year of the Carter Administration, when arrangements were negotiated for dealing with maritime, fishing, air piracy, tourism, cultural and academic exchange, and similar issues between the two countries. In both cases the talks were broken off as a result of U.S. resentment against Cuban military activities in Africa.

The time is ripe for another try. In June 1980, the Cuban government showed its desire for negotiations by offering for the first time in two decades to negotiate without preconditions. (Until then, Cuba had insisted on lifting of the U.S. embargo as a precondition; also, it had ruled out any discussion of Cuba's overseas military presence.) The United States should resist the temptation to gloat about Cuba's internal problems and should seize the opportunity for fresh diplomatic initiatives aimed not only at livable bilateral relations but at a stabilization of the security of the entire region. For example, U.S.-Cuban cooperation could reduce the frequency of terrorist acts, including air or naval piracy, and could more effectively interdict the flow of narcotics and guns. The likelihood of yet another chaotic boat exodus from Cuba would be reduced by direct contact. Regular exchanges about the policies and intentions of the two governments would enhance both their own and the region's security.

Search for Stability

In today's circumstances, the United States has no need— indeed, can no longer afford—to center its Caribbean policy on containment of Cuba. Rather, it must be free to concentrate on the more basic threats to U.S. interests arising from instability within the region. It is no news that the enormous inequality of power and wealth makes the Caribbean states highly vulnerable to the United States: for example, the 5 percent of U.S. imports that came from the Caribbean in 1976 included 94 percent of all exports from the Bahamas, more than two-thirds of all exports from the Dominican Republic, Haiti, and Trinidad and Tobago, and more than 40 percent of all exports from Jamaica, Belize and the Netherlands Antilles—to name a few (see Table 2). What *is* news, perhaps, to most North Americans is that virtually all the countries of the Caribbean are likely to continue to export their

71

people—and hence a portion of their persistent poverty—to U.S. shores. The greater the economic distress and political instability in future years, the greater the pressure of emigration will be, to say nothing of the jeopardy to established, "safe" sources of bauxite and oil.

A U.S. policy that can serve U.S. interests in the Caribbean, then, will lay less relative emphasis on military affairs. Politically, it will seek to promote stability through normal working relations with Cuba, the principal state of the region. Beyond this, its essentials can be summed up in three words: migration, development and diversification.

The Migration Problem

The Caribbean, along with Mexico and Central America, must take a prominent place in the rethinking of U.S. immigration policy that is under way. Although a comprehensive solution to the immigration problem cannot be expected except in the long term, some specific questions should be explored without delay. For example: Can there be better coordination among the European and Western Hemisphere countries that have received Caribbean migrants in the past, so that migrants can know better where they will find homes and jobs? Can temporary U.S. work visas be more widely used, so that more Caribbean people can find work in this country without becoming permanent residents?

And, finally, is it proper policy to accept Cubans, but not Haitians, as political refugees, when both alike have fled not only from economic hardship but also from authoritarian political systems? (The current law defines a refugee as a person who has suffered persecution, or has well-founded fears of persecution, on account of race, color, creed, national origin or political beliefs. This applies, in principle at least, to all countries.) The authors think not. If the U.S. government is going to refuse political asylum to the Haitian boat people on the ground that they are economic refugees, then it should do the same to the recent Cuban arrivals. Conversely, if the United States is going to grant asylum to the Cubans on the ground that many of them have experienced persecution or have well-founded fears of persecution should they return to Cuba, then it should also grant asylum to the Haitians. There are few signs that such equal treatment will be given. After much lobbying on behalf of the Haitians by the Congressional Black Caucus and a few concerned individuals, the U.S. government in 1980 granted the Haitian boat people who arrived in the United States before October 11 special status. But in January 1981 it moved to expel newly arrived Haitians while permitting most Cubans to stay. The correction of this injustice to Haitian refugees is long overdue.

The Basic Solution: Development

There can be no long-term solution to the problem of Caribbean migration to the industrial world except through the development of Caribbean economies and the maturing of their political institutions. Thus it is of the highest importance that the United States take a more active part in helping the Caribbean countries provide a decent life for their peoples. In addition to improvements in the aid programs in which the United States already participates, several additional measures should be taken.

First, substantial international assistance should be available to encourage Caribbean countries to revive their efforts toward regional integration, since most of the smaller units cannot hope to attain satisfactory standards of living as independent states. Regional schemes have failed repeatedly, partly because they were too ambitious. CARICOM, however, made some important strides in the late 1970s in harmonizing tariffs and coordinating development projects. Efforts should be made to build on these beginnings.

A second economic need is to increase lending to Caribbean countries on concessional terms (that is, low-interest, long-term loans). This is especially important at a time when most of their payments balances have been hard hit by the rising cost of imported fuel. And since the benefits of regional integration are so unevenly distributed, with the poorer countries lagging behind, an important U.S. objective should be to increase the inadequate resources of the Caribbean Development Bank, which continued to increase its loan activities all through the 1970s and gave special attention to the needs of the less-developed countries of the region.

Thirdly, the United States could provide special trade facilities, commodity earnings-stabilization arrangements and tariff concessions to the Caribbean countries—perhaps in a broad agreement comparable to the Lomé Convention of 1975 between the European Economic Community and most of the former European colonies throughout the world. As one specific example, products manufactured from sugarcane residues, such as paper and wallboard, could be imported into the United States under lower tariff schedules, thus raising the region's income from what is still its main source of employment—and reducing the pressure to migrate to the United States.

A domestic corollary of this economic development approach is the need to ease adjustment for import-competing industries and their employees within the United States. Both justice and politics will require that wherever U.S. jobs are lost as a result of tariff concessions, generous adjustment assistance should be provided.

Diversification: A Trend to Be Welcomed

Finally, it should be observed that the economic policies sketched here also imply further diversification of the economic and political relations of the entire region. The United States has nothing to fear from this trend; indeed, it should welcome it. Just as this country should not be the sole prop of struggling Caribbean economies, so also we should not wish to monopolize their trade or other relations. The direction of the diversification already evident holds no sinister implications. As Table 2 indicates, the United States and Western Europe dominate the region's trade. Even in Cuba's case, after the Soviet Union, the main trading partners are Japan and Spain. This transition away from traditional dependence on a single outside power is likely to gain momentum in the coming decade, especially in the English-speaking countries and the Dominican Republic, whose

Bridgetown, Barbados: 31 percent of the country's exports go to the United States, 14 percent to Ireland

governing elites wish to diversify their international relations without any implication of hostility toward the United States.

Among near geographic neighbors, Venezuela's widening role is particularly notable. The Venezuelan government (more recently in conjunction with Mexico) has moved to assist Caribbean countries to bear the burden of increased energy prices and has begun to supply its own political alternatives to Cuba's influence. On the world scene, Caribbean countries rely heavily on their membership in the UN and other international organizations. These bodies provide a shortcut to world diplomacy for small states unable to afford a large diplomatic service. Caribbean nations' support for the New International Economic Order is part of this larger effort to secure international assistance, broaden their range of international relations, and maintain and enhance their sense of national sovereignty.

The United States and its allies will remain important to the

Caribbean because only they have the capital, technology and markets so vital to the region's future, and only they have the open, competitive, pluralistic political systems to which nearly all Caribbean countries adhere or aspire. Diversification, then, is not a code word for anti-Yankeeism. Rather, it is a way to provide a more solid collective foundation—more politically defensible within each country—for the international relations of Caribbean states, as an alternative to hegemony or imperialism from any quarter.

Toward a Sustained U.S. Policy

"Many of our own major mistakes, indeed," wrote Assistant Secretary of State for Inter-American Affairs Adolph A. Berle, Jr., in 1939, "in this hemisphere have been due more to the fear of European domination than to any desire to increase the area of our territory," or, he added, to serve the perceived needs of U.S. firms. Substitute "Soviet and Cuban" for "European" and that statement takes on a disturbingly timeless quality. The Caribbean is often ignored at higher levels of the U.S. government. When it does receive high-level attention, the cause is usually political and strategic: a fear of some other power's real or alleged involvement in the region. This narrow preoccupation explains the cycle of alternating indifference and panic that has marked U.S. Caribbean policy at most times during this century.

The alternative proposed here could be described as a policy of sustained middle-level attention. It should flow from a presidential decision but it could best be implemented, gradually, and modestly, under the leadership of under secretaries and assistant secretaries in the relevant departments. This approach is to be preferred to sporadic presidential attention, which in the past has so often treated the Caribbean not as the home of 30 million neighbors but as one more square on a global chessboard, or else as a counter in the game of domestic politics.

The Carter Administration, at different times, illustrated both these approaches. President Jimmy Carter's initial decisions concerning the region considerably improved U.S. relations with virtually all countries in it. The later obsession with containing

Cuba once again relegated the Caribbean to the geopolitical chessboard, obscuring its underlying problems and complicating efforts to promote Caribbean development.

The Caribbean can never again be regarded by the United States as no more than a traditional strategic frontier. It has become inextricably intertwined with the future of this country, all the more as Europe recedes from the region and as so many people from the region call the United States home. Its people and its affairs will not leave the consciousness of U.S. citizens or the agenda of the U.S. government. But it remains to be seen whether the necessary efforts, sustained from one presidential administration to the next, will be made to build an adequate U.S. policy for the Caribbean and to break at last the old cycle of indifference and panic.

Talking It Over

A Note for Students and Discussion Groups

This pamphlet, like its predecessors in the HEADLINE Series, is published for every serious reader, specialized or not, who takes an interest in the subject. Many of our readers will be in classrooms, seminars or community discussion groups. Particularly with them in mind, we present below some discussion questions—suggested as a starting point only—and references for further reading.

Discussion Questions

The authors argue that the involvement of the United States in the Caribbean is not a matter of choice but of necessity. In what ways is the Caribbean important to the United States? Has U.S. policy in the past reflected this significance?

The Cuban revolution did not succeed in reducing Cuba's economic dependence on foreign powers. Is this evidence of the inability of Caribbean countries to overcome their historical dependence or of the failure of Marxist ideology to bring about real economic change?

The U.S. government fears that Caribbean governments may by "swinging to the left." On what is this fear based, and how valid is it?

What responsibility, if any, does the United States have for the continuing underdevelopment of the Caribbean? Can or should we assist Caribbean countries in reducing their dependence and fostering their development?

Colonialism, slavery, and export-production were for years trademarks of the Caribbean. In what ways has this legacy influenced contemporary Caribbean societies?

Should the United States treat Caribbean immigration as a form of U.S. aid to the region? Should Haitians be granted political refugee status in this country? What changes, if any, should be made in U.S. immigration policy?

Should U.S. military or diplomatic concerns override U.S. concern with human rights in the Caribbean? Is there room in U.S. immigration policy for the concept of "economic refugee"?

READING REFERENCES

Beckford, George L., *Persistent Poverty: Underdevelopment in Plantation Regions of the Third World*. New York, Oxford University Press, 1972. A compelling analysis of Caribbean economies and a Caribbean scholar's view of the region's underdevelopment.

Domínguez, Jorge I., *Cuba: Order and Revolution*. Cambridge, Mass., Harvard University Press, 1978. Possibly the most comprehensive history of 20th-century Cuba, this book concentrates on how Cuba has been governed.

Domínguez, Virginia R., *From Neighbor to Stranger: The Dilemma of Caribbean Peoples in the United States*. New Haven, Conn., Antilles Research Program at Yale, 1975. Monograph examines the five main migrant flows of Caribbean people to the United States and explains the differential treatment each has received.

Knight, Franklin W., *The Caribbean: The Genesis of a Fragmented Nationalism*. New York, Oxford University Press, 1978. This study of five centuries of economic and social development in the Caribbean emphasizes the problems of nation-building in an area with many people and few resources.

Lowenthal, Abraham F., *The Dominican Intervention*. Cambridge, Mass., Harvard University Press, 1972. Based on extensive interviews with a wide range of Dominican and American officials, this study examines in depth the 1965 U.S. intervention in the Dominican Republic.

_____, and Fishlow, Albert, "Latin America's Emergence: Toward a U.S. Response." HEADLINE Series 243. New York, Foreign Policy Association, February 1979. Changing realities in Latin America require new U.S. policies, these authorities assert. Useful as regionwide context for study of the Central America-Caribbean subregion.

Lowenthal, David, *West Indian Societies*. London, Oxford University Press, 1972. A comprehensive study of the non-Hispanic Caribbean, showing the extent to which the Caribbean past still actively affects the region.

Mintz, Sidney W., *Caribbean Transformations*. Hawthorne, N.Y., Aldine Publishing Co., 1974. Although pan-Caribbean in scope, the book sheds particularly interesting light on the development of Jamaican, Puerto Rican and Haitian societies.

Naipaul, Vidiadhar Surajrasad, *The Middle Passage: Impressions of Five Societies: British, French and Dutch in the West Indies and South America*. New York, Macmillan, 1963. The Trinidadian novelist of East Indian origin presents a poignant picture of the dynamics, ironies, contradictions and difficulties of social life in the Caribbean.

Sharpe, Kenneth E., *Peasant Politics: Struggle in a Dominican Village*. Baltimore, Md., Johns Hopkins University Press, 1977. Shows the interpenetration of local-level politics and the international economic system.

Singham, Archibald W., *The Hero and the Crowd in a Colonial Polity*. New Haven, Conn., Yale University Press, 1968. This detailed look at the rise of Eric Gairy as a charismatic leader serves as a background for analyzing the recent Grenadian revolution.

Smith, M. G., *The Plural Society in the British West Indies*. Berkeley, Calif., University of California Press, 1965. Offers picture of Caribbean countries as societies based more on conflict than social cooperation.

Stepan, Alfred, "The United States' interests and the Instruments of foreign policy and the World (1979), Vol. 58. American relations with special se Puerto Rico.